Terrance Pennington's

Play-by-Play

Coaching You Through His Weight-Loss Formula

Terrance Pennington's
Play-by-Play
Coaching You Through His Weight-Loss Formula

By Terrance Pennington

Disclaimer: the Publisher and the author make no representations or warranties with respect to the accuracy or completeness of the contents of this work and specifically disclaim all warranties, including extended by sales or promotional materials. The advice and strategies contained herein may not be suitable for every situation. This work is sold with the understanding that the Publisher is not engaged in rendering legal, accounting, health, medical, or other professional services. If professional assistance is required, the services of a competent professional person should be sought. Neither the Publisher nor the Author shall be liable for damages arising here from. The fact that an organization or website is referred to in this work as a citation and/or a potential source of further information does not mean that the author or the Publisher endorses the information the organization or website may provide or recommendations it may make. Further, readers should be aware that internet websites listed in the work may have changed or disappeared between when this work was written and when it is read.

ISBN-10: 1522790160
ISBN-13: 978-01522790167
Library of Congress Cataloging-in-Publication Data
Printed in the United States of America

Published by:
The TP Experience
P.O. Box 355
Lebanon, TN 37087

Phone: 615-513-5555
E-mail: Terrancepennington@outlook.com
Website: www.TheTPexperience.com

Interior Design by: Ann Haney

Editing by: Tracy Johnson

Book Cover Designer: Mike Turbeville

ACKNOWLEDGMENT

One of the greatest characteristics I pride myself on is the ability to always be humble and take the golden nuggets of experience and knowledge from others. This journey to help people finally understand the mindset and formula needed to reach their goals would never have happened without the love, sacrifice, and guidance from so many positive people in my life. In the process of writing this acknowledgment, I truly was able to appreciate how blessed I am to have had these wonderful people cross my path.

I want to thank my loving parents, Henry and Donna Pennington. There are no words I can put together to express how grateful and lucky I am to have two parents that will literally do anything to make sure I succeed and reach happiness. There was never any doubt in anything I attempted, and they always picked me up if I failed. Love you guys. And to my brother Kevin who is my biggest cheerleader—I hope I made you proud, little bro—thanks for always having my back. I know my grandmothers who spoiled me and always made me feel loved are watching from heaven. To my extended brothers and sisters Athena, Tasha, and Shane—we spent a lot of time together growing up and shared so many memorable moments; memories that I will take to my grave. I will always be your big brother.

I want to thank my wonderful hometown friend, Kalim, for his friendship and brotherhood. Thank you, Javoris, for being the big brother I never had. You taught me so much about what is cool and what is not. Your positive influence was a big factor in my development from a boy to a young man. Thank you, my high school buddies and teammates: Jason, BCY, Malcolm, and so many others for making my high school experience enjoyable. I am glad I found good guys to mimic and follow. P.T.A. all day! Jason, you are a person I model myself afterwards because of your willingness to do what is best for you, such as transferring to Georgetown. Thanks for the e-mail that sparked my vision to create a team.

Here's to my University of New Mexico football family: Gabe (R.I.P), Tony, DonTrell, Big Hater, Scott, Claude, Cook, Hump, Bo, Jerrell, Rudy, and everyone else that made college so damn fun. Quincy, I am proud of your accomplishments and your drive to be successful after football; you are an inspiration to me. Thank you for your help and friendship when I was going through my depression phase after ending my NFL career. To my friend, Byrd, thanks for the deep conversations we had and never making me feel judged. You are a great friend to so many, and we are all blessed to know you. I am so grateful my father recommended that I attend the University of New Mexico because I met some awesome coaches there. Thank you to Rocky Long for offering me the opportunity to be a Lobo. Your encouragement to believe in myself changed my life forever. I have met a lot of coaches along the way traveling through my football career, but there were no coaches like you, Bob Bostad. You turned me into the war daddy I am today. Also, thank you for the "fat camp" we did together at 6 a.m. to help me get into better shape. Thank you for pushing me when I was lazy and never giving up on me. I mimic your intensity and approach in everything I do in life. I forever owe you my life.

During my NFL experience with the Buffalo Bills I met my brother from another mother; his name is Walt. From the very first day with the Bills I was asked by other teammates if I had a brother, because there was a guy on the team that looked similar to me. You know, Walt, that we clicked the day we met, and you will forever be considered my family. Thank you for your support and sympathetic ear when I needed you. You always know how to make me laugh when I am down. Love you Walt.

To my mentor, Ambrose—you took a lost guy straight from the NFL under your wing and molded me into the strong-minded man I am today. Your ability to get the best out of me day in and day out is amazing. Your relentless drive is inspiring to watch. Your motivational words that always turn my blood into fuel to light my soul on fire have pushed me to new levels I never thought possible. I know, for sure, deep down in my heart that this journey would have never happened without you. From every book you told me to read, to the demanding expectations you set for me, you helped me to finally see my true potential. My wife always tells me that she loves when I have phone conversations with you because you inspire me to dig deeper.

Jimmy, I thank you for seeing this vision before it was ever birthed in my mind. You always preached to me that I should write my story, but I always felt so overwhelmed because I had never written a book. I want to greatly thank Kavin for believing in me and introducing me to Renee. I remember my very first conversation with her (and her deep New York accent) and wondered how she could help me. Renee, I thank you for the attention and guidance I needed to guide me through this writing process. I know that sometimes I moved at a snail's pace because of my low level of confidence, but you always pushed me to keep going until this book was finished. Tracy, I thank you for editing my content; I am sure, at times, it gave you a headache.

Lastly, I want to thank my wife, Sabrina. Thank you for sacrificing our quality time together so I could write this book. Day in and day out you were there for me while I was sitting up in bed writing. When doubt clouded my mind, your loving and encouraging words came at the exact time I needed to hear them. I hope you are proud to be my wife. I love you!

DEDICATION

I dedicate this book to anyone that has a deep burning desire to become the person they are destined to be. This is for the person that keeps getting up after repeated failure. How we deal with failure determines our success.

Contents

Introduction 7
Chapter 1: The Journey 8
Chapter 2: My Household 11
Chapter 3: Growing Pains 16
Chapter 4: Welcome to Compton 18
Chapter 5: My High School Days 22
Chapter 6: New School and New Zero 26
Chapter 7: Facing Adversity 28
Chapter 8: The College Years 32
Chapter 9: The Spark of Belief 35
Chapter 10: The Combine Invite 39
Chapter 11: My NFL Experience 42
Chapter 12: Depression Through Transition 45
Chapter 13: My First Failing Attempt 49
Chapter 14: Finally Found My Purpose 53
Chapter 15: I Am In My Own Way 56
Chapter 16: First Two Weeks On My New Journey 62
Chapter 17: Change Happens And Is Sometimes Needed 66
Chapter 18: Three Keys To Sustain Motivation 72
Chapter 19: How I Created The Formula 79
Chapter 20: Plan 82
Chapter 21: Commit 88
Chapter 22: Win 95
Chapter 23: Repeat 99
Chapter 24: How To Become Great at Weight Loss 103
Chapter 25: Adapting Through The Process 108
Chapter 26: Measuring Your Activity 116
Chapter 27: "You Look Great" Trap 124
Chapter 28: How Does The Journey End? 128

Introduction

I was once in your shoes, struggling time and time again to lose unwanted pounds. Every day I looked in the mirror and was disgusted with myself because I knew that I deserved better. I experimented with lots of different diets, only to fall flat on my face. After my journey of ups and downs, good and bad days, and smiling and crying days, I finally learned how to acquire what I really desired. I ultimately became the type of guy I had always admired. People always ask me what secret or golden nugget I have that explains how I lost over one-hundred pounds. I try to give them advice, but in the end it is never enough time to equip them for the gruesome journey. It's extremely hard to offer a complete blueprint in a five-minute conversation. So, I finally decided to write down my formula for success. I wanted to thoroughly breakdown solutions to the problems we all share.

Oftentimes our "why" is not strong enough to carry us through the storm. Many have failed to lose weight because they have applied the completely wrong approach to attacking problems. Upon reading this book you will learn your true purpose in achieving weight loss. You will choose more successful methods that will provide different results—results you can finally control and be proud of. I challenge you to truly let go of past failures as well as your feelings of denial and frustration. Let me show you the true Terrance Pennington and how I was able to change my life forever. It's time to erase all of your previous failing attempts. Now you can press the reset button and begin your passage with a fresh, new start. Use the journaling at the end of the chapters to help you gain more insight into your unique journey. If you want change to happen, then remember *you* must change first.

Chapter 1: The Journey

You have accomplished great things in your life, but you just can't complete this journey. You know once you finish the journey, it will forever change your life. This journey has caused people to go into depression and, worst of all, settle for defeat. Millions of people have begun this journey and millions have failed. The journey I am referring to is the challenge to lose enough weight to reach inner peace—the inner peace we are missing by being unhappy with our health, decisions, habits, and self-image. We have attempted this journey so many times and have always ended up with the same results—not finishing to the end or losing our focus. This time, before starting your new challenging journey, I would like to share some great news with you.

You are not the reason why you can't finish this ultimate challenge. You do not need super powers or special gifts as though you are a golden child. There are two reasons why we fail time and time again to beat this gruesome trial. The first is that attacking the journey with the wrong approach will slowly kill you. We take the approach of hoping and wishing for an easy route that will cause no pain—looking for the new pill or gimmick that will lead us down the yellow brick road—to experience the lifestyle change we all want and desire. We must go through times of struggle, sacrifice, change, commitment, steady focus, and hard work. These characteristics that sound so harmful are, in fact, the keys to your success. Developing these characteristics will carry you further along your journey.

The tough times you go through make you appreciate the journey once you reach the finish line. You will experience the highs and the lows. Always remember there is no progress without struggle. Starting your journey without a proven system is the second reason why the journey may defeat you. So many of us (including me) started a weight-loss journey with a guessing formula—choosing to guess how much food to eat daily and choosing to guess how to properly exercise. In the end, this has left us with failed results.

Following a system that uses guessing will frustrate you in the long run. The feeling is like driving to a friend's house for the first time without the correct directions. You will deplete your gas tank, waste time, and begin to pull out your hair because of the frustration. If you have felt this way, then I am glad you chose me to be your navigational system. I will point you in the right direction, but you have to drive the car. Your effort to press on the accelerator and make the correct turns will get you to the final destination of your journey. If you are willing to do the work, then take the car out of park and let's ride.

Journaling: What's Your Story?

Chapter 1: The Journey

1. What have you accomplished in your life that took time, commitment, sacrifice, and change?

2. Do you follow a proven system to reach your weight-loss goals? ___Yes or ___No. If not, then explain why.

3. Have you failed many times (as I have) with your past methods and attempts? ___Yes or ___No. Share your story.

4. Are you finally ready to learn how to beat this challenge that is holding you back from your ultimate happiness? ____Yes or ___No. Explain why or why not.

Chapter 2: My Household

Our childhood environment and habits play a significant role in the person we become. As children we have very little control over our environment and are forced to adapt to our surroundings. I have formed habits from people that raised me or from those I hung around with daily. My story, which I'm sharing with you, explains why I struggled with losing weight on my journey. As you look back upon your own upbringing, hopefully you can identify your strongholds.

I was raised by two loving parents in the heart of Los Angeles, California. My mother, a kind and thoughtful person, has always loved serving others and making them happy. I believe I inherited this personality trait from her. I feel so good when I help people develop and grow into their potential.

My mom was raised in Louisiana, and she knew how to cook very well—maybe too well. This had a large impact on me being such a big kid. Our family was a huge fan of rich and flavorful pasta meals. My great grandmother cooked a big feast at all times when she welcomed visitors to her house. As a child, my mother picked up the habit of cooking a surplus of food. My mother only knew how to cook for an army, not a family. I remember my father always asking, "Honey, why do you cook so much food?" She would answer, "I didn't know it would be so much. You can always take some for lunch tomorrow."

There was never a shortage of food in my house and because of this I grew to learn how to eat a lot until my stomach felt like it would burst. There were times I ate so much food I had to lie down like a stuffed turkey. I usually couldn't move for the next few hours. If anybody knows me well, then they can tell you that my favorite food was and still is macaroni and cheese. My mother cooked that for me at least twice a week, and I would consume it like I was in one of those pie eating contests. I hung around my mother a lot growing up, so I guess you can say I was a big momma's boy. We went shopping together and every time it felt like torture. My mom was just like most women; she would try on every pair of shoes or dress in the store. It was okay at the end of the shopping trip because she always bought me some kind of ice cream or treat to reward me for my patience.

Growing up, my mother was my biggest fan. She attended all my sport games when I was a young pup. I could hear her loud screams over everyone's voice, yelling out, "Let's go BIG-T!" My mother came to every practice and game, no matter what the conditions were. If it was cold and raining or blistering hot, she would still be there supporting her baby boy. Many family members on my mother's side passed away from cancer, and I am sure that scares her every day. She has been through some tough times, but those periods made her faith in God stronger every time. My mother is a strong survivor of the horrible battle of ovarian cancer. I always admired her for pushing through and never giving up on herself.

My father grew up in the dangerous neighborhoods of South Central Los Angeles in a household with eight brothers and sisters. He was known as the leader in his family. He was the backbone and problem solver. I call my father the "fortune cookie" because he always had the right words to say when I came to him for advice. He learned to be very tough so that he could protect his brothers and sisters from the neighborhood bullies. My father grew up with rough uncles who encouraged him to be tough by always punching him and wrestling with him. I don't think he enjoyed those childhood experiences very much because he never used that "you need to be tough" approach on me.

One thing for sure is that my father made it a priority to spend time together as a family and take family vacations. I can recall my father insisting that the family eat dinner together every night at 6 p.m. so we could interact. Yes, that all sounds nice and dandy, but not so much when it was down to the last point to win the basketball game—my friends, as well as the whole neighborhood, heard my mom calling out to me, telling me it was time to come inside for dinner. Of course, that was a time when kids actually played outside. I would get so angry at dinnertime because I had to go inside and end my fun. Most times I complained, telling my parents that all my other friends didn't have to eat with their families. My father would give me one of his harsh looks, and I knew nothing else needed to be said. Sometimes I tried to be slick and eat fast so I could go outside and continue having fun with my friends. My father would outwit me and tell me I could not leave the table until everyone else was done eating their dinner.

My father was the rock of the family because he knew how to deal with the stressful times. He always found a way for the family to make it through the storm. There were times when money was low and my parents told us we would have a "red beans and rice week." Buying rice and beans in bulk was very inexpensive, and we were often able to make them last the entire seven days. My parents didn't share their financial problems with me; they wanted me to focus on my studies and sports. I know my father lost his job at one point, so that must have added to their financial troubles. Luckily, with my mother's cooking experience from Louisiana, she knew how to make all those simple meals we shared absolutely wonderful.

My father played sports all of his life and was good enough to earn a scholarship from the almighty Stanford University. If I don't add the "almighty" part, he will kick my butt. He lived a short career in the NFL because of injuries. He never talked much to me about his college days or playing football in the NFL. I'm guessing this is because he was not content with how his career ended. Although he was a football fan, he never pushed the sport of football onto me. He cared more about education because he knew that education was guaranteed and the sport side wasn't. I can hear him saying, "Terrance, commit to your education so you can succeed in this hard world we call life." My mother told me that my father almost didn't take her to the hospital when she was in labor because the Dallas Cowboys were playing. It was and still is a state of emergency when his Cowboys play on television. Everything stops and nothing else is more important. Growing up, I was as competitive as my father. We were so competitive that I decided to fall in love with his team rival, the Philadelphia Eagles. I chose the team just so we could enjoy the competition when watching the two teams play against each other every year.

When I was growing up I can remember my dad being a workout junky. He worked out early mornings and after work. He played pickup basketball games every Saturday with his friends. He also played flag football for a few years on a team called the "Raw Dogs." These were a bunch of old guys that were former athletes, trying to relive their playing days. Their wives cheered them on but also prayed they wouldn't get hurt and have to miss work the next day. Since my dad was with his friends on the weekends, I usually spent this time with my mom. If I could change one thing from my experience with my father it would be spending more time together to develop my inner toughness—teaching me proper technique and understanding the game of football. Overall, my father did the best he could raising my brother and me to grow up to become strong leaders. Only the Lord knows how difficult it can be living in violent neighborhoods surrounded by bad influences on every corner.

My brother Kevin is my best friend and understands me more than anyone else. He has played a huge role in my life. For the first ten years of my life we never went outside to play with others because my mother feared we would be influenced by gang members. So, Kevin and I played video games, watched cartoons, and played in the backyard. Our backyard was our playground. My father poured cement over the grass and made us a basketball court with a ten-foot pole. My brother and I spent many hours on that court, since that was the only outside area where we were allowed to play. Kevin was the "daredevil" in his younger years. I often heard him called "crazy Kev" because he was the opposite of me regarding his conduct in school. He was the kid that did not care about getting in trouble—from stabbing a boy in the back with a pencil, ditching school, or just following through with anything and everything that sparked his brain as a confused, young kid. That boy received lots of whooping's because of being so bad in school, and after a while, it felt like the norm. My mother would make an excuse to go to the store because she hated to hear my brother cry from getting his spanking.

Growing up, I wasn't exactly an angel either. I was just a little smarter than my brother and I feared getting caught. As I see it now, it was good for my brother to be as disciplined as much he had been or his constant bad choices could have damaged his life forever. He was my little brother, a.k.a my son, during my NFL-playing years, and I felt it was my duty to take care of him. My increased salary made it possible for me to take some of the burden off my parents in supporting him. Both of my parents made so many sacrifices for us—it felt really good to be able to step up to plate and help out.

Journaling: What's Your Story?

Chapter 2: My Household

1. Did your parents consistently practice healthy habits during your childhood? ___Yes or ___No. Share your story.

2. Do you want to be a better example for your kids or future kids? ___Yes or ___No. If so why?

Chapter 3: Growing Pains

My parents put my brother and me through private school so we could learn core values. They sacrificed their wants and needs to pay for our tuition each month. My mother always told me she wanted to buy a drop-top convertible with her hard-earned money but thought our education was more important.

Throughout my elementary years I was the person that constantly talked in class, quite often receiving a pink slip—in other words, detention. I was, for the most part, a pretty good student but my mouth was something I could never shut. One thing that I could never hide was my love for talking. My hardest challenge in life was keeping my mouth shut in class. I remember my mother constantly putting me on punishment for getting "excessive talking" pink slips. The funny thing is that both my mother and father are motor mouths—I was just following in their footsteps. It is also interesting that even though my constant chatting was once viewed as a curse, it has now turned into one of my greatest gifts.

Our house was *the* family get-together house for holidays. Every Thanksgiving, Christmas, New Year's Eve, and birthday was celebrated by having our whole family at our home. My family was bigger than the average-size family. It looked like a house full of football and basketball players. Most of my extended family members were overweight or morbidly obese, and they loved to eat at our house. Remember that my mother cooked for an army so she had no problem having enough food to feed everybody. I never saw their size as a problem, and I thought it was just normal for us. They always seemed to be in a great mood whenever food was present.

The members of our household mostly watched basketball or football on television. Baseball never caught my parents' interest; they thought it too slow. I played all types of sports in my physical education classes during my earlier school years, but I suffered a huge embarrassment after my very first time playing baseball. It felt like it was yesterday (when I was nine or ten) when the batter hit a pop fly. The ball soared in the air and was coming my way. I yelled out to everyone, "I got it, I got it!" The next thing I knew I was laying on the ground because I misjudged where to hold my glove to catch the ball from the sky. The baseball landed on my head, and I experienced the worst headache ever.

From that moment on I told myself I'd stick with basketball. I played basketball for park leagues and earned the name of "Baby Huey." My size made it easy for me to dominate on the court. I was so much taller than everyone, and I could easily grab the rebound without jumping. I can remember my mother yelling from the stands, "Jump Terrance!" In my opinion, I didn't have to, but I guess it was just the foundation of laziness being built.

As an adolescent I was not an aggressive big guy. After running over a little shrimp of a kid on the court, I would put my hand out to help him. My mom would yell out, "Don't pick him up!" So, I guess you can say I was the soft marshmallow instead of the belligerent pit bull. That mentality surely got me exposed once we moved to Compton, California.

Chapter 4: Welcome to Compton

My brother and I seemed to be growing bigger and at a faster rate than the other neighborhood kids. My parents decided it was time to look for a larger home. While on those house-hunting excursions, I was amazed at the idea of having my own room. I remember my dad coming home one evening and telling my brother and me that we would be moving in less than a month. We were so excited! Then, suddenly, all plans changed when we learned that we could not actually move in until the following month. Unfortunately, we had to be out of our current house way before that timeframe.

Facing the prospect of his family being homeless, my father decided to find a hotel room for us. He did just that and we stayed there for the first two weeks of the month. You can bet that Kevin and I really enjoyed swimming in the pool every day. The cost of living in a hotel was damaging my parents' savings, so we left and split up for the remainder of the month, until our new house was ready. My mother, brother, and I stayed at my grandmother's house and my father lived with his mother.

The time had finally arrived, and we were able to move into our new house. And, yes, Kevin and I both had our own rooms, which made us very happy. Our family liked the new home, but the street we lived on was kind of another story. See if you can picture a half-mile of road with split personalities. Well, our end of street was very family oriented. Neighbors were friendly and helpful, and we played with their kids. The road on the other end of the street was gang infested and very dangerous. As you can imagine, my brother and I were not allowed to visit that end of the street.

Moving to Compton was definitely a culture shock for my brother and me, as we transitioned from a soft private school to a rough and tough public school. Many know Compton for its high crime rates due to violence and gang activity. I was only eleven years old when we moved there, so I didn't yet understand what the city was actually like. As they say, things changed from zero to one hundred really quickly. Everything just seemed so different. The kids were more aggressive and the teachers let a lot of things slide—no way that would have happened in my old private school. My brother and I were finally allowed to play outside in the front yard because my father put up a basketball net on the roof in front of our garage. This started the evolution of being the new kids on the block. Most of the neighborhood children came to our house because we were the only ones on the block who owned a basketball court. We thought we were rock stars.

One of the guys that I became very close friends with was named Kalim. He grew up four houses down from me—we clicked instantly. We went to the same school, so we played basketball together during lunch. He was a gifted athlete with a competitive edge. He was not tall, like me, but his athleticism made up for his lack of height. I used to be amazed at how high he could jump or how fast he could run. We played on basketball and football park leagues together, and my parents treated him like their own son. He was the star of the teams I played on and definitely received most of the attention. I can remember hating to lift weights with him because I would feel so embarrassed at how much stronger he was than me—even though I was probably twice his size. My father would say at times, "Call Kalim to see if he wants to work out with us," and I would lie and say, "He is at his grandma's house." I know it sounds terrible that I lied to my father, but as a young kid I wanted my father to be proud of me.

I always felt that my father would view me as "less than" because I was not strong like Kalim. Instead of asking Kalim what he did to be so strong, I decided to run away from my problems. This was nothing, however, compared to entering the seventh grade at one of the roughest middle schools in Compton—Enterprise. Enterprise was located in one of the worst areas of Compton where gang activity was (and still is) extremely high. Since I was a very nice kid, I had never been in a fight in my life and never had enough confidence in myself to know that I could protect myself. Riding on the school bus was one of the worst experiences because the guys who were in cliques all rode together. I often got slapped in the back of the head, and I remember being scared to fight back because I feared how bad it would hurt to fight them all. I was so much of a punk I would sometimes walk home, which was extremely far, so I would not have to face them. Never once would I tell my parents because I knew I would be looked upon as being the snitch. There's one thing about growing up in Compton—you never want to be called the snitch.

Since I was overweight, I was often teased for how my belly poked out and how my chest sagged. Hearing that you have a chest like a girl in front of other girls will crush any young man's self-image. I often tried making jokes back at the kids so that the pressure would be taken off of me. When you are always being teased you definitely learn fast to have thick skin. My friend Kalim was more of a ladies' man, and I just sat back and wished that girls paid attention to me like that. So, I just focused on trying to get good grades and playing sports at the park leagues to sustain my happiness.

In my last year of eighth grade, I decided to play football for my school, instead of playing at the park league. All the coaches were excited about me coming out to try out for the team. Our first practice was focused on conditioning because the coach wanted to get us into football shape. We all lined up on the goal line and mostly ran up and down the field for the entire practice. I was so out of shape that I was not able to finish the running drills. Have you ever started breathing so hard that you thought your heart would pop out of your chest? Well, I thought my heart was going to pop out of my chest and through my shirt. The pain I experienced with the lack of oxygen flowing through my lungs was excruciating. I never went back to practice and told my father I just wanted to play basketball. That day started my pattern of quitting when I felt out of my comfort zone.

Journaling: What's Your Story?

Chapter 4: Welcome to Compton

1. Did you experience being teased because of your weight problem at school? ___Yes or ___No. Share your story.

2. How did the teasing affect your self-esteem?

3. Did you have a friend you admired? If so, what trait did you admire most?

Chapter 5: My High School Days

After eighth grade graduation I had my eyes set on attending a private school in the City of Watts, California. For those of you who have never heard of Watts, it made Compton seem like Pleasantville. I attended an all-boys private school, directly next to the projects. A majority of the students, from very tough upbringings, came from those projects. Sometimes that school felt like a warzone. I didn't mind the thought of feeling unsafe, though, because I had protective friends surrounding me.

I had my eyes on playing tackle football my first year of high school. I invested time with my father and Kalim in our garage, consistently lifting weights. I was ready for the challenge because I wanted to make my father proud. I had butterflies in my stomach because I had never even played one down of tackle football. In California's school system, tackle football starts at the high school level.

Being a heavy kid, I was not able to play in the Pop Warner little league because I could not make the weight requirements. Since I was bigger and heavier than most, I would have to play with those several years older than me. I was neither mentally nor skillfully prepared to compete with older children, even when we were the same weight. So, my parents decided I needed to wait until high school to play tackle football.

Waking up the morning of my first day of high school I was ready to put on my very first football helmet. During the time when I was playing football at the high school level, Nike Sharks were the most popular shoes with kids. Well, my parents didn't believe in buying me high-dollar shoes, so I had to wear my father's old cleats called Riddell's. These were the old dusty cleats my father wore during his league park flag football games with his buddies.

I remember sitting anxiously on the bench in the locker room with my stomach turning like clothes in a dryer. I didn't know what was expected of me and how it would feel getting hit at full speed. The only thoughts that ran through my mind were the hard hits I saw during NFL games on television. As I walked into the locker room I began to watch the other guys putting on their football gear. I sat on the bench with my pads in front of me looking lost like a kid trying to put a puzzle together. I had no idea where to put the butt pad or how to correctly buckle up my chinstrap. Realizing I was running out of time, because coach was expecting us on the field any minute, I had to figure it out fast. Then I heard the coach yell out, "Let's go—everyone out on the field!" I grabbed one of the guys in the locker room and asked him to show me how to put on my football pads correctly. I lied and told him the pads I was used to wearing were quite different. I didn't want to be seen as the new rookie. I hurried up and put my cleats on and ran onto the field.

My heart was pounding and fear was really starting to set in. We started stretching, and I looked down and noticed my damn shoes were on the wrong feet. I laughed to myself but couldn't switch them because everyone would notice; we all were stretching in a big circle. So, I had to go through the torture of my pinky toes being smashed in the sides of my shoes for the first twenty minutes of practice until we received a water break. After the water break it was time to strap up and then we began with hitting drills. Everyone was excited to show the coaches and each other how they were the hardest hitter on the team.

When my name was called and I had to go up against a big senior lineman, all I could say to myself was, *"Don't show your weakness in front of everyone."* We got down into our stance, looked each other in the eyes like two pit bulls ready to fight. Clenching up one of my fists, I was ready to hit him as hard as I possibly could. The whistle sounded and we clashed into each other with my eyes closed. I was chopping my feet trying to push him backwards and the whistle blew again for us to stop. To my surprise the drill was over and I didn't feel any pain. At that moment I knew I could play tackle football.

The first two years of football in high school were fairly boring because I never played a snap in any game. I was not consistent with going to practice either. Missing practice only hurt me because I never developed my skills. I remember after the games rubbing dirt on my football pants on my way home so it looked like I played the game. I laugh now thinking about it because I really took my time making sure the grass stains looked real.

Sports were not going well for me because I never fully committed to improving my skills. Besides showing up to practice, I didn't really know exactly how to get better. I hated going to practice because I knew at the end of it we had to run laps around the field. It was a fact—my love for football was slowly fading away. I was not experiencing the typical enjoyment the sport lends to an athlete—the gratification of running down the field after scoring a touchdown, feeling stronger and more experienced, and basking in the glow of the recognition received upon completing an excellent play. I was experiencing plenty of pain but not much pleasure.

I was succeeding with my grades, however. School happened to be a breeze because the expectations were not set as high as they had been at my previous private school. I remember being in the ninth grade and teachers having to teach the meaning of a pronoun and a verb. It was sad, but I just sat back in my chair and enjoyed the easy ride.

Football athletes who didn't pass the SAT in order to enter college were serious problems in our athletic department, and my parents didn't want me to become a victim. They felt the school was not challenging me enough, and that I wouldn't pass the SAT. My grades were good—obviously too good, because my parents yanked me out when I came home with all A's and one B on my report card. My parents thought it was best to move me out of that school and transfer me to a more prestigious school called Bishop Montgomery.

Journaling: What's Your Story?

Chapter 5: My High School Days

1. What was your most embarrassing day in high school? Share your story.

Chapter 6: New School and New Zero

Entering a brand new high school in a totally different environment, I began eleventh grade. Attending Bishop Montgomery was a big culture shock to me. For one, it was fifteen minutes from the beach and very diverse. The first week of school I saw my fellow students rolling into the parking lot in BMWs and top-of-the-line vehicles. I grew up in neighborhoods living with African Americans and Hispanics. Attending school alongside whites and Asians was not the norm.

In the eleventh grade I stood six-feet-five-inches tall and weighed well over 300 pounds. Since I was such a big kid I stood out, and everyone knew I came to play football. The football program did not win one game in the past season. You can say they went defeated. Everyone in school saw me as their hero—the one to swoop in and help them to finally win a game. I saw myself as the zero because I had zero number of plays executed on the field. Little did they know that I had never played a snap in any game.

We had our first day of practice, and I remember meeting the head football coach, Jimmy Sims. Coach was in great shape, looking like he just stepped off stage from a bodybuilding competition. He always wore shorts that reached his mid-thigh, and I guess it was to show off his big quads. He had a sense of humor like no other coach I ever met. The guys on the team constantly teased Coach and he would just laugh back at them. He definitely humored us with his jokes, but when it was time to get serious, he made a certain face that made you almost shit your pants.

Our first day of practice was all about getting into football shape. I just prayed for the strength to make it through. It felt like the time during practice went into matrix-style-slow motion because it seemed like we ran forever. I actually thought for a second that he was punishing us. So, of course, with me being the out of shape one, I was dragging at the back of the pack. I'm sure that my new teammates looked at me and thought, "How is this guy going to help our team when he can't even finish the conditioning drills?" I felt so low and embarrassed that I just wanted to disappear.

When I got home I went straight to my room and stayed there, thinking of how I would ever be able to show my face again. I had so much pressure on my shoulders to help the team get out of its defeated slump; I had no choice but to go back to practice. After time and time again of being the last person to cross the finish line during the conditioning drills, I told myself that I had enough. I was tired of being laughed at, being looked down upon, and feeling embarrassed amongst my new teammates. I made up my mind that I would not go to another practice and I would quit football forever. That night lying in bed was the longest night ever because I knew I had to face my father the next morning and tell him I wanted to quit.

Chapter 7: Facing Adversity

The next morning came and my father told me to get up and get ready for school. I told him that I didn't want to play football anymore. He walked into my room, sat on my bed, and asked me why. Like any kid I said, "I don't know." I really did know, but I couldn't tell him the real reason. After he asked me over and over again, I finally told him the truth. He looked at me and said, "Quitting will be the easiest thing to do ever in life. You are better than that. This is just an area you need to work on." Like any good father, he made me continue playing football. I looked at him with that sad puppy-dog face, hoping he would change his mind, but all he said was, "Get up and get ready for school. You *will* be going to practice." I went back to practice and eventually as the days went on I was okay with being the last person in the back of the pack. I just accepted the fact that running was not for me.

On the days we had extreme conditioning I sat in my classes, frightened the whole day. I wouldn't eat most of the time because the thought of running took my appetite away. My first year, as a junior, at Bishop Montgomery I didn't play football because I was not developed enough with my technique as an offensive lineman—so I rode the bench. I learned a lot that year and sharpened my skills so I would be ready for opportunities during my senior year.

After my junior campaign season ended, I was able to watch my senior upper classmen receive full sport scholarships to great colleges. Seeing their parents' faces filled with joy and happiness motivated me to give my parents the same feelings. My senior year finally arrived, and I knew I had to make big noise on the field if I wanted to earn a football scholarship. There was no way that my parents could afford to send me to college, so I knew I had to make the best of the opportunity. I busted my tail the summer before my senior year, hitting the weights and spending extra time on the field working on my skills. I began loving the game of football because I started to play in the games and finally became part of the team's success. The joy of being a major contributor as well as receiving confirmation from my teammates was one of the best feelings I ever experienced. For the first time in my life I earned the first team All-C.I.F. honors, which meant that I was one of the best linemen in our conference. That's not bad for a kid who only started playing football in his first year of high school.

As you know, with success comes confidence. My senior year I was a fan favorite at school and grew to have lots of friends. I talked to girls on the phone until late hours of the night. I knew that football was a huge reason for my increased level of confidence. No matter how much confidence I had, I was still very self-conscious of my body because I was not happy with how it looked naked. There were many times I would not go with friends to pool parties or water parks because I did not want them to see my big stomach or love handles. I bet the person that came up with the name "love handles" was a skinny person. I never knew a soul that fell in love with the fat rolls on the sides of their stomach. I was so caught up in their opinion of me, I didn't want to fall back to those old memories of being teased for being the fat boy.

There was one girl in my high school that I had a crush on. We had a best friend type of relationship. Yes, I was put in the friend zone, but I didn't mind because I got to hang out with her a lot. The worst part about it was that she would talk about the boys she had crushes on and they were always thin guys. She frequently told me what a great guy I was, but I felt she was only saying that because we were such good friends. This is a typical scenario many heavyset boys have to endure when they are overshadowed by others with more fit bodies. I always felt that most young girls were more interested in showing off their good looks and trim bodies to their friends and boyfriends. They'd rather do that than find a person that makes them happy and feel good inside. That always bothered me, but instead of changing my body, I decided to settle with my inner pain.

I enjoyed the parties and popularity that football brought to my senior year. My football talents improved but my grades were going downhill. I figured as long as I got a scholarship and passed the SAT, I would be fine. Boy, was I wrong on that one. I was not aware that grade point averages determined the minimum SAT score required in order to become eligible to earn a college scholarship.

The best and worst day was graduation day. My entire family attended my graduation. Everyone was all smiles until we arrived home. After retrieving the mail, my mother proclaimed (quite loudly), "Terrance, I have your report card." When I heard those words I knew instantly the graduation fun was over. My mother opened the envelope and stared at those poor grades. Her smile turned into a frown. I saw her light-skinned complexion on her face instantly turn red. She looked at me with so much disgust on her face; I knew I had let her down. There was no way I could make it to college with those grades. So, I had to take the SAT again and try to get a higher score so I could be eligible. Otherwise, I'd have to attend community college. I knew I couldn't let my family down, so I had to buckle down and study with extreme focus.

After taking the test, waiting for the scores to come in the mail was the longest period in my life. We finally received the SAT scores, and I scored high enough to be eligible to enter my first year of college. I chose to go to the University of New Mexico. I couldn't tell you where that was on the map of the United States, but my father really loved the offense line coach Bob Bostad. He was a stern coach that preached about how important technique was with my position of an offensive tackle. Coach had an enthusiastic approach to get his guys fired up to play. His fire was something my father thought I needed to get the most out of me. My father knew that I was raw because I didn't really have much football game experience. I only played my senior year in high school.

It was amazing that the day finally arrived for me to leave home and start my new life. I knew I was starting a new chapter, and I also knew I made my parents proud. Leaving my family and all my friends was the most bittersweet part of the whole experience. Both my close friend and football teammate, Jason, and I earned full scholarships to the University of New Mexico—at least I knew I was not going to this new and foreign place alone. We became roommates our first year living in the dorms. I was away from home and starting my journey in becoming my own man. Living on my own in college meant I had to wash my own clothes, budget my money, get up on time to get to class, and manage countless other activities. Living with Jason helped a lot because he was a great planner, neat, and very laid back. I still don't know how he was able to deal with my snoring for a whole year. Sorry for your long sleepless nights, buddy.

Journaling: What's Your Story?

Chapter 7: Facing Adversity

1. Have you ever had to face adversity? If so, once it was over, were you happy that you went through the storm? Share your story.

____
____
____
____
____
____
____

2. Was there a person in high school that you had a crush on and you wish they would have chosen you? ___Yes or ___No. Share your story.

____
____
____
____
____
____
____

Chapter 8: The College Years

The first day of football practice was exciting because I was now at the big-boy level. I was a college athlete and couldn't wait to play. On the first few days of camp, the members of the freshman class were the only ones on the field being educated on the plays. This gave us a few days of learning so that we wouldn't be so far behind knowing the plays when the vets arrived. The problem, though, is that there was a low number of linemen. Basically, I had to run every play, with no break in between. I almost collapsed from exhaustion.

No one told me about the high altitude in Albuquerque, New Mexico, and it was hard for me to breathe in enough oxygen. As you know from my past, running was not my favorite activity. During our first practice I knew if this would not end soon, they were going to have to call the paramedics to carry me off the field. The air was thin and it seemed like I could not get sufficient air in my lungs. Practice was finally over and I knew I had a long camp ahead of me.

The vets came the next few days and, of course like any competitor, I had tried to measure up to them. They were bigger, faster, and stronger. It became clear to me that I had more work to do on my body. I went through the first year of college refining my technique and learning a lot about myself as a person. Basically, my mother had taken care of me my whole life—washing my clothes, cooking my food, and cleaning up most of the mistakes I made. That was absent in New Mexico, so I had to make the right choices or I would have to pay for them.

After my first year of football we did not make it to a bowl game. I was out of football from the end of November until the middle of January. All I did each and every day was eat and sleep. I enjoyed that time off and didn't exercise once.

The football team had a mandatory meeting our first day back for the winter semester in January. In the locker room before our meeting I heard a few of the guys saying that Coach wanted us to weigh in. I knew I would be in deep trouble because the late-night eating at my favorite restaurants almost every night was going to show on that scale.

We all were told to march toward the training room and step on the scale. There was a line and it seemed like that line was moving very slowly. My anxiety was growing stronger and stronger because I had no idea how much I would weigh. My turn was finally up and the numbers read across at 352 pounds. I gained twenty-one pounds in six weeks and my eyes were big. The guys knew I would be in big trouble, and I had no idea was about to happen to me, since I tipped the scale at that number.

After our meeting I was called into Coach Bostad's office, and I knew for sure he was going to chew me out. He was very calm and told me to see him every morning at 5:30 a.m. until I got my weight down to 325 pounds. I would rather have had him yell at me then tell me to get up early every morning to workout with him. Four other guys participated in that morning workout program. We called it "Fat Camp."

The following days were spent in heavy one-hour cardio workouts with the Coach, attending my classes in school, and then returning to the facility to workout with the team. I think I ate salad and chicken nuggets every day until I took the weight off. By far, that was the hardest regimen I had to sustain in my life. Going through that process and losing over twenty-five pounds helped me to become a better athlete. I was able to run longer at practice and not get so winded. Laterally, I moved much more easily and more quickly. During the process of losing those twenty-five pounds I wanted to quit football, of course, but going through it until the end was one of the best things that I could have done for my football career.

The next two years I played behind the upper classmen and did not begin to earn a starting position until my junior year. I had an "okay" junior campaign but learned a lot through the mistakes I made on the field. I realized how much better I needed to become to get a shot at playing in the NFL. To be totally honest, everyone in the locker room talked about wanting to play in the NFL and I truly didn't believe in my own capabilities of having a legitimate chance.

Going into my senior year I was looked upon as a leader on the team by my other fellow seniors. We had the biggest offensive line that year, and our offensive star running back, DonTrell Moore, was ready to take us to the Promised Land. DonTrell was an over 1,000-yard rusher all four of his stunning career years. As a running back, he broke every school record. Our team was packed with experienced seniors—if ever there was a chance to be undefeated, that was the time.

Journaling: What's Your Story?

Chapter 8: The College Years

1. Who was the person who pushed, motivated, and inspired you to bring out the best in you?

Chapter 9: The Spark of Belief

My only goal for my senior year was to have a good year and enjoy it playing collegiate football. I did not receive any awards prior to my senior year, so I guess you can say I didn't have any high expectations for myself. Before our season started we had a team meeting, and our Head Coach said something that changed my life forever. Coach was very straightforward and told us the honest truth even at times when we didn't want to hear it. I respected Coach because I trusted that he had the best interest at heart for every player.

During the meeting we listened to Coach speak about how our team could make history by going undefeated, due to all the great talent we had in the room. I was sitting in my chair, half listening—probably thinking about something else at the time. My mind tended to wander off during these meetings. As I sat there, I heard Coach say, "We have two senior linemen that will be playing on Sundays, and we need them to dominate and set the tone for the other players on the team."Ryan Cook was our center and everyone knew he had a true shot to make it in the NFL. The only other senior was me, and when I heard that statement I was in shock—just the thought of him believing I could play in the NFL! When the meeting ended I went home and just sat on my bed and thought to myself, *"If Coach thinks I have a shot to make it to the NFL, then why not make a serious effort?"*

I never told Coach that his speech changed the path for my life. So many kids go through life with no one believing in them and telling them that they can become something special. Coaches have a lot of impact on their players. I know that many parents try to protect their children's hearts by building them up with praise. However, sometimes they tell their children want they want to hear, not always what they need to hear. We, as athletes, listen and hold onto what our coaches tell us because, I believe, coaches show their honesty more readily than parents. Coaches often tell us things we don't want to hear, but as players we appreciate the truth, whether it is good or bad. That player must understand, with no doubt, that the coach has only the best intentions for him or her to be their best.

Once my belief changed as to who I could potentially become, my mental frame of mind instantly changed as well. I began to invest more time in watching film and being focused on getting better during practice times. In the past I always looked at practice as something I needed to get through instead of an opportunity to get better for that day. I know it sounds horrible but it was the truth. I went through the season playing my best football, and I can say I was proud of my efforts.

The season ended and it was time to focus on my one-shot opportunity of making the NFL roster. Honestly, I can say that I never expected to be one of the guys drafted, but I just wanted a shot, even if it was through free agency. To my surprise, I was invited to a small named all-star game for senior football players to show off their skills on tape for NFL teams to observe. I was so excited to be picked to attend the all-star game and to be an inch closer to my goal of getting on an NFL roster.

This was not your average big-name Senior Bowl in Mobile, Alabama, with the shining lights. The budget for this all-star game in Mississippi was so small we had to change clothes on the field before and after practice. Our hotel was very low star, but I just had my eyes on having a good game to showcase my skills. It was raining extremely hard throughout the game, and we had to show off our best work in the muddy terrain.

My last game with New Mexico was played in San Francisco. The weather was very similar, with heavy rain. I learned how to adjust my techniques halfway through that game, so I would not slide all over the field. Later, at the all-star game I made sure I used the same techniques I learned in San Francisco. With every step I took on the muddy field I planted my feet hard on the grass. This way, my cleats could grab enough grass to stop my feet from sliding. I noticed other guys were slipping because they were trying to make quick, sudden moves. I slowed down, and doing so helped me to have more body control. While my opponents looked unorthodox and silly, I appeared calm and cool.

Guys from several colleges played in that game, all with one goal: to beat their opponent so they could get a shot at the National Combine in Indianapolis, Indiana. If you were invited to the combine, you were one step closer to having all thirty-two teams view you as a prospect. The NFL combine is *the* job interview for the NFL teams, so it's possible to have your name called out on national television on draft day.

I played very well in the all-star game and was later invited to another all-star game that received more attention from the NFL scouts. This was the East/West All-American all-star game in Las Vegas, Nevada. Invited players were on the radar, but the scouts wanted to be able to see more tape in order to make the best decision when drafting players for their team.

Performing well in front of the scouts was my ultimate goal, but doing so caused me to become very nervous and anxious. I was letting the fear of failure get inside my head. I knew it was time to call my mentor, my dad. He stated the conversation by saying, "You were not expected to be at that all-star game and so you have nothing to lose." He told me to go out there and have fun and fight for respect. During the practices I battled against top guys and kicked butt. I was very proud of my courageous performance and truly felt that the videotape/film viewed by the scouts would give me a good shot at performing at the Combine.

Journaling: What's Your Story?

Chapter 9: The Spark of Belief

1. Who is the person that believes in your goals and dreams?

2. Have you started your weight-loss journey? ___Yes or ___No. If not, then explain why.

Chapter 10: The Combine Invite

After the all-star games were completed, the waiting game began—waiting to receive an acceptance letter. Many letters and phone calls were coming in from agents offering to represent me. My father was adamant about making sure I hired an agent that truly held my best interest. I visited several agents, but the one that stood out the most to my father and me was Harold Lewis because of how honest he was with my evaluation. He told me what I needed to hear instead of what I wanted to hear. He was candid about what he had heard regarding my performance grade from NFL scouts. He thought I might be a last-day draft prospect, at best. Other agents tried to impress us by explaining how much money was made by the other players they represented. We drove in fancy cars to expensive restaurants. My father and I were more concerned about what the agent could do for me and my career. Once the decision was made to sign with an agent, the process to improve my skills began.

My last semester of school I made a decision to stay home and train at a well-known facility for professional athletes called "Athletes Performance" (AP).The facility was ten minutes from my home in California, so it was very convenient. This would allow me to go to training and focus on being the best athlete that I could be. With the support of my mom and dad I could focus and commit to my sport without the worry of having a job and paying monthly rent.

The trainers at AP coached me on how to run a forty-yard dash, bench press 225 pounds with as many reps as possible, and perform field agility drills. Offensive tackles ran ten yards, at the most, every play, so I bet the site of us running the forty-yard dash was quite hilarious!

As I was driving home from training I received a call from my agent telling me I was invited to the National Combine to display my talents to all thirty-two teams. It was exciting and nerve-racking at the same time. I felt mounting pressure to do well—everything truly was on the line here. I trained hard every day at the training facility until the day came for me to fly to Indianapolis for the ultimate interview.

My mother and I headed for the airport, and I was ready to perform at my highest level. I flew out of LAX, which is by far one of the biggest and busiest airports ever. After I got out of the car and kissed my mother goodbye, I turned around and saw a bus full of kids jumping into the Southwest baggage check line. All I could say to myself was, "God, are you serious right now?" With the line moving so slowly I glanced at my watch every couple of minutes. I finally realized I was going to miss my flight. Panic settled in and I prayed they could get me on a later flight so I could check into the hotel and get off my feet. Luckily, the check-in lady found a later flight for me. I tried to calm down by telling myself that this was just another test. I understand that God takes us through these tests so we can use the test as a testimony. Can you imagine the feeling I had sitting in the airport knowing I had to tell my agent I missed my flight, while trying to keep a calm and positive mind?

I arrived at the hotel, saw all the top athletes, and came in contact with NFL head coaches. It was breathtaking. I was told that during our three-day stay at the Combine we would meet with coaches in their hotel rooms to have videotape-recorded individual meetings. The top guys were getting notes all throughout the day for setup times for their interviews. I felt very small and unimportant because I did not receive one single interview. It's not that I was in denial about being a top NFL prospect. However, what I couldn't was why no one (and I mean not *one* team) wanted to talk to me. I thought I had something to offer to the right football team. Again, I just told myself that I could only control what I could do, which was to perform well when it was my time to show my value.

The days were long, and after three grueling days of mental and physical focus, the Combine came to an end. I enjoyed the Combine experience, and every time I see the next class of players competing at the Combine, I always go back and reflect on my time there in Indianapolis.

After the draining four months of consistent training and steady focus, draft day finally arrived. My agent told me I may be between a fifth- and seventh-round pick. Of course, we all hoped for the best, but I wanted my named to be called on national television so my parents could live and celebrate in the moment of their hard work and sacrifice. The last day of the draft I received a phone call from the Buffalo Bills asking me how I was doing. I told them, "I'm doing great now that you have called." They told me they were drafting me in the seventh round with the 216th pick. As I was talking on the phone with the Head Coach, Dick Juaron, I saw my name flash across the screen. In the background, my mother screamed so loudly, I jumped. Seeing my dad smile and be the proud father I always wanted him to be definitely was my proudest moment of being his son.

Once I hung up the phone and realized how cold the weather was in Buffalo, New York, my attitude slightly shifted. After all, I am a warm-weather kid from Los Angeles, California, where there is no snow. I knew that I needed to be happy for the opportunity to play in the NFL—a feeling not experienced by the majority of athletes. Actually, only 1 percent of college athletes make it to the NFL.

Chapter 11: My NFL Experience

If you asked my old high school teammates whether or not I would ever be part of the NFL, they would, with no hesitation, tell you that would never happen in my lifetime—never to the young kid that almost quit because he hated the thought of running and looking embarrassed in front of his teammates—never to the guy that truly only played three years of football on the field in his senior high school year and last two years of college. The first year of my football career I learned a lot about how to become a pro. I was educated on how to take care of my body, study, practice, and carry out the duties held by an NFL player. My NFL experience shows that anything is possible as long as you keep pushing through the tough times and have a strong belief in yourself. What a luxury it was to shower my family with gifts and not have to look at my receipt when I pulled money out of the ATM. I enjoyed the first-class airline flights, as they allowed me to stretch out my six-foot-seven-inch body on the plane and ride comfortably.

Even though I enjoyed playing in the NFL, I did have one major challenge. One of the hardest trials was staying under my maximum weight. In the NFL we are given a maximum number we can weigh, and they are strict about it—so strict that a player could be fined four-hundred dollars for every pound over the limit, every day, until the weight falls beneath the maximum number. My max number was 338, and staying under this number toward the end of the season was the hardest. At this point in time the coaching staff shortened the practice time and the intensity so we could heal our bodies from the long season of occurring bumps and bruises. Since less energy was expended during those end-of-season practices, I also burned fewer calories. I never had to pay any fines by going over my max weight, but I was damn close. Money is one of the greatest motivators. Can you imagine being fined for every pound you were overweight? I bet you would be motivated to do what it takes to get in shape and lose those unwanted pounds.

One of my craziest moments in the NFL dealing with weight was what I experienced two days before reporting to camp. I was four pounds over my weight, and I did not want to pay the fine or be looked upon from my coaches as out of shape. During the last two days before my weigh-in I decided to drink only water and not eat a thing for the remaining two days before reporting to training camp. It was the longest two days of my life. I couldn't think about anything else besides eating food. I wanted my cravings to stop. I lasted two days without eating and reported to camp under my max weight. I would definitely never recommend this practice to anyone, but it saved me money in the long run.

My last two years in the NFL was mentally draining because I had to deal with injury after injury. My last year with the Atlanta Falcons I experienced a torn pectoral muscle. My last year with the New York Giants I could not heal the arch pains in my left foot. After months of battling the injuries, I decided to discontinue the sport of football. I wanted to move on because the journey started to become physically very painful—painful because I could not perform on the field without having sharp pains in my foot.

It came time to face one of the hardest challenges of my life—the decision to try to continue to rehabilitate my injuries or walk away from the NFL. Deep down I realized that I was ready to start a new chapter in my life and walk away from the game. It was the most difficult decision I ever had to make for my life. Overall, I am appreciative for every moment I had playing the game of football. It taught me many wonderful lessons about how to fight for my goals and to have the discipline it takes to become great. The one thing I knew for sure was that all of my past experiences would help me to become successful in the next chapter of my life.

Journaling: What's Your Story?

Chapter 11: My NFL Experience

1. Were you ever on top of your game in any field (career, sports, health), and it was taken away? ___Yes or ___No. Explain what happened.

2. How did it affect your self-esteem and confidence? Share your story.

3. Are you still affected by the experience? ___Yes or ___No. Explain why.

4. Are you currently at a crossroads and not sure what the next step is to take on your journey? Or are you completely sure about the next step on your journey? Explain.

Chapter 12: Depression Through Transition

For the most part, I am a happy-go-lucky guy. I seldom let lows bother me because I fought through so much adversity growing up. I left New York and moved back home to Nashville, Tennessee, to live with my parents. I knew I needed to spend some time there until I got back on my feet and figured out my next plan in life. Now that my football career was over, I felt stuck and didn't know what to do to earn a living. This fact hit me hard to my core. I felt like I lost control over my life—something I was definitely not comfortable with. You have to understand that when you have money, for the most part, it helps to put control back in your corner. They say money is not needed, like oxygen, but it's pretty damn close.

While playing in the NFL, I became accustomed to a certain type of lifestyle, and then all of a sudden it was gone. During that time of my life I cared about what others thought of me. I let others' opinions run my emotions and change how I felt about myself. I can honestly say that two things were the very best part about me being a professional football player: 1) my family and friends were proud of my accomplishments, and 2) I had the resources to help my family. With that said, you can probably understand how not having that feeling could destroy my world. I was judged my whole life because of my big-kid size, so those opinions wore on me. Living the life as an NFL player felt like a dream.

When my career was over, I opened up my eyes each morning only to feel as though I was in the middle of a nightmare I could not wake up from. Have you ever got so down on yourself that you feel like no one will understand? Isolating ourselves may be one of the steps we take when we feel no one will understand our situation or pain. I really did feel alone and shut off from everyone else, and I didn't have anyone close to me I could trust to express my deep painful feelings to. I also alienated myself because I was tired of reliving the story every time someone would ask me why I stopped playing football. The problem with doing that is I let my own negative thoughts and fears tear down my confidence. I did not reach out to others that could have instilled hope or confidence in me, helping me to make a successful transition.

There was a time when looking at my bank statement brought a big smile to my face. After football, I was scared to glance at a bank receipt. My back account was dwindling (with no deposits), and I knew I had to do something or I would become a victim of the NFL-broke statistic. The sport of football was what I ate, breathed, slept, and thought about for the last eleven years, if you include my time spent in college and high school. I truly understand what military personnel go through when returning to civilian lifestyle after previously being brainwashed. The reason I use the word "brainwash" is because as an NFL athlete we are trained day in and day out to dedicate all our time and effort toward the sport of football. As professional athletes we are accustomed to having a schedule six to seven days a week. After my career ended, I felt like a bum with no direction or purpose.

During the first year out of the NFL it was hard for me to watch any professional football games on television. Whenever I thought about my NFL career, angry thoughts consumed me. When I did watch the games on TV, I said to myself, *"I am better than THAT player. Why does HE get to play NFL and enjoy life while I sit here in misery?"* I noticed myself watching the games with so much hate in my soul, not because I was mad at the guys playing, but because I was more upset that I could not be on the field enjoying life as an NFL athlete.

Instead of watching football on television, I chose to run errands or do practically anything to keep my mind off the sport. I purposely did all my chores, grocery shopping, or anything I could think of to distract me from thinking about football. All of my family members are football fans, so my parents wanted me to spend time with them and watch the games. I always made up excuses why I couldn't.

During my depression stage, the only true friend I felt I had was food, because food had never let me down. Food always made me smile when I was down and was always available in my times of need. Since I had no schedule, I watched television all day and snacked on chips and sweets. I've always been a night owl so, normally, I stayed up late watching television.

Throughout the night watching food commercials, I would become inspired to throw on clothes to drive to any fast-food spot that was open. I had no awareness of the habit I was forming, but I guess I didn't care because the habit felt so good. Staying up past 3 a.m. every night was my routine and waking up late was my life. There was no purpose in my life and sleeping away time was my comfort zone. I preach that having a purpose in life is very meaningful for the human spirit. Waking up day after day with nothing exciting to look forward to wears on the human mind.

After being home for a few months doing nothing productive, I knew I had to get out of my rut. I never had a job in my life, so I didn't even know where to begin to look for one. Creating a resume and prepping for an interview was a joke.

Many times I pondered falling back on my opportunity to become a police officer. My major in college was criminal justice, and I enjoyed the study of criminals. I always thought that being a police officer was something that would keep my attention after my football career. I enjoyed being around the guys in the locker room, so I figured I'd get that same type of team feeling being an officer with other officers around me.

Becoming a police officer and having the possibility to move up in ranks because of good work was similar to sports. Helping people is a trait I get from my mother, and I knew that giving back would give me the satisfaction that my work would be appreciated. I applied for the Tennessee Police Department and prayed I would get an opportunity quickly to enroll in the police academy. I knew I would have to pass a physical test to become an officer, so I figured I'd better get back to the gym.

Journaling: What's Your Story?

Chapter 12: Depression Through Transition

1. Have you ever gone through depression? ___Yes or ___No. Share your story.

2. If yes, how did it affect your life? Share your story.

3. Did depression affect your weight gain? ___Yes or ___No. Share your story.

4. Do you isolate yourself when you are feeling down? ___Yes or ___ No. If yes, share your story.

Chapter 13: My First Failing Attempt

I went through the same process as the average person when trying to get into shape. I woke up my first morning and stepped on the scale. Now, understand that I had not stepped on a scale since being in the NFL. I also did not even own a scale, so I had to go to the store and purchase one.

All of this time I guessed I was close to my playing weight of 325 or so. I jumped on my new scale and the number read 369. I jumped off immediately—clearly I was not ready to digest that number. I was certain it was a mistake, so I moved the scale over to the other side of the bathroom floor, hoping it was wrong because the floor was uneven. The scale read 369 again. Shocked, I just sat down on the floor. I couldn't believe I let myself go and climb to that weight.

I got up off the floor and went to the grocery store to buy healthy food. Doing this was really tough because all the tasty cookies, cakes, chips, and other foods I was used to buying were staring me in the face. I felt like they were saying, "Terrance, I know you want me. Put me in your basket." The struggle was real, and I knew I had to maintain my focus. I went down every aisle trying to figure out what good tasting low-calorie foods I could buy. I decided to buy my favorite cereal, Fruity Pebbles, because on the box it stated there were 110 calories per serving.

I knew the basic rules of keeping my calories down low to lose weight. I bought several boxes of cereal and several gallons of milk. I checked out at the counter looking like a big kid with all those boxes of cereal. The clerk probably thought I was feeding a daycare facility full of kids.

My nutrition game plan was ready to go, or at least I thought it was. We live in a society that puts so much emphasis on caloric intake, so I figured that's the avenue I needed to take. I ate Fruity Pebbles cereal for breakfast, lunch, and dinner. Of course, my serving size was a bit different than what was suggested on the box. I ate the cereal out of a huge bowl with a large amount of milk. So, I ate the same cereal day in and day out. I thought it was the best diet ever, until I stepped on the scale to see if my weight had changed. Boy, was I in for a rude surprise. This time the scale read 371. I almost threw it against the wall because I was so angry. The confusion on my face was like no other. I knew I couldn't give up, so I had to find another approach.

During my college days I remember watching girls eat salads in order to lose weight. So, I went back to the grocery store and stocked up on salads and ranch dressing. Do not judge me. I love ranch and I knew if I ate salads, I would lose a lot of weight. I piled ranch dressing onto my food like people put salt on theirs. I put it on French fries, pizza, spaghetti, and any type of meat. I knew as long as I could add ranch dressing to a salad, I would be good to go. I was not sure if the dressing would help or hurt me, but I knew ladies lost weight eating salads, so I thought I would give it a try. I put myself on a time-eating program. I ate my big salad with chicken or shrimp at 2 p.m. and 9 p.m. I figured by cutting out meals, I'd also cut calories.

My mornings were torture because I was so hungry. I knew I had to stay disciplined and stick to my plan if I wanted to lose weight. Many days I lay in bed and slept until it was time to eat. I felt even more depressed using this method of losing weight. I would step on the scale and lose a few pounds a week until results stalled.

I understood that the beginning was always the hardest part in any new journey, but this particular journey was heartbreaking. I struggled at times, trying to find my motivation to get my butt up and head to the gym. My workout regimen was even worse than my diet.

During my years of playing in college and the NFL I always had coaches that depended on me to show up. Of course, there are times when we, as athletes, do not feel like working out. When you have no choice but to show up, it makes it easier to achieve perfect attendance. It is no different than when someone goes to work every day—no matter how that person feels, the supervisor still expects you to show up.

My workout program consisted of working on the cardio equipment and lifting weights. I never enjoyed the cardio machine because I got extremely bored and felt like I wanted to kill myself if I stayed on it another minute. It was so boring that I always found myself getting off the machine before I had completed my scheduled time. I spent many football-playing years lifting weights a certain way—in order to become big, fast, and strong. The problem was I wanted to become lean and small. I would, of course, lift heavy weights and perform the same exercises I learned from football. You must understand that lifting the same way for more than fifteen years of my life was nothing to look forward to when arriving to the gym. It may feel like working for the same company and doing the same job for so many years. Eventually the excitement leaves and the job is an activity of just going through the motions. This attempt was not giving me the results I desired, but I knew I had to keep pushing through the tough times.

Journaling: What's Your Story?

Chapter 13: My First Failing Attempt

1. When was your first failing attempt on your weight-loss journey?

____
____
____
____
____
____
____

2. What was the craziest diet you ever attempted?

____
____
____
____
____
____

Chapter 14: Finally Found My Purpose

It had been a little over a month and I had not received one call or e-mail about being accepted by the police academy. My motivation to eat right and exercise was slowly dying by the day. My salads were boring to eat and I fell back to my old habits. Being in the house all the time with very little social life, I started to have the itch to go out and meet some people. The only people that I had contact with were my parents and a few people at the gym. I decided to ask the front desk guy for places to go to hang out and have a good time. He told me to talk to the general manager of the gym, a guy by the name of Walt Williams.

Walt was a short, muscular guy but had a big personality. Walking into his office and introducing myself, I asked him for places to hang out that would be fun for a guy like me. He invited me to go out with him and his friends. After being cooped up in the house for the past few months, it felt really good to socialize with somebody.

Later that evening I started to have doubts about going out. Looking at the mirror at my size 6xl shirt, I felt disgusted. I didn't want to stand Walt up, especially since it was our first time hanging out. I surely did not want his first impression of me to be a flake.

The night out was fun and I met some good guys that were in the fitness field. They drove new cars with shiny new rims and they all made quite an impression on me. There was no doubt in my mind that they were all doing well financially in the fitness industry. My reality was that there was no way I could bring in NFL paychecks working in a gym, but I really didn't want to live a lifestyle that would have me struggling paycheck to paycheck. After observing them, I noticed how confident they were and I admired them.

On our way home Walt and I had a conversation that changed my life forever. We talked about my playing days in the NFL and how he would have loved to play on the professional level. For some reason he made me feel like I could trust him, and I shared with him my troubles of trying to transition from the NFL life. I shared that I was trying to get into the police academy but with no luck yet—I was still waiting for their call. He mentioned something I honestly can say never crossed my mind. He asked, "Have you ever thought about being a personal trainer? You definitely have the exercise history, and with your experience playing in the NFL you can help many lives." I quietly sat back because I was thinking of why I never thought of being a trainer before. I asked him about the process of becoming a trainer, and he told me to go online and earn an accredited certification.

After he dropped me off at my house, I rushed upstairs and surfed online, looking up different certifications. The conversation with my new friend definitely peaked my interest but negative thoughts stormed in my head—thoughts like, "*You cannot be a personal trainer because you are too fat*" and "*Who is going to listen to you with your stomach hanging over your belt?*"

The next day I went to the gym to talk to Walt about which certification I should purchase so I could work at the gym with him. He got out of his chair and walked me around the gym to the office of a guy by the name of Ambrose Leburu. Ambrose stood about five feet nine inches on a good day but his presence and confidence matched the size of a giant. He was a smooth talker and a great motivator. He advised me to sign up for the National Association of Sports Medicine which provides one of the best personal training certifications available.

We talked for about an hour, and he truly motivated me to think that I could become successful in the fitness industry. He was someone who could talk a homeless guy out of his last dollar. He was great with his words and made anyone feel like they could do anything. Before exiting his office, he gave me advice that would forever change my life. He said, "If you really want to help others, you must first be the example." For the first time in a long time I went home with a sense of purpose I had not felt since playing in the NFL. Later that evening, I purchased the certification package and waited for my textbook and other tools to arrive in the mail.

At the University of New Mexico I was never enthusiastic about reading books for classes or doing any type of school work. The first day I received my books in the mail and started my journey in becoming a certified personal trainer, I was so excited. This new feeling I had was something special. I studied day and night, learning chapter after chapter. Learning about the anatomy of the body and how the body performs had my full attention. I finally understood about nutrition and why I was not losing weight with my weight-lost nutrition practices. For example, I didn't know sugar turns into fat, so all those bowls of Fruity Pebbles were just helping me to add on the pounds. I learned that the high fat content in the ranch dressing was building more fatty acid, which in turn helped me to put on more weight. Eating only two times a day was not good because I learned I was slowing my metabolism.

The knowledge I was gaining from this certification process was mind blowing and made me feel slightly better about why I failed to lose weight with the approach I was using. In just under four weeks I finished the course and was ready take my test. People say when you are passionate about something it doesn't feel like work. Well, I can say I was not sure that training was my passion at that particular time, but I knew the yearning to learn was new to me. I became addicted to this new way of learning because I finally grew to believe that I could truly begin my fitness journey and actually hit my goals.

In order for me to become a certified personal trainer to help others I had to pass my exam at an offsite location. To my surprise, I did not feel nervous at all. I knew the information from the book like the back of my hand. I arrived at the test site ready to go.

The test instructor stopped me in my tracks and informed me that my CPR card was invalid. At this point, both my nerves and blood pressure started to rise. My CPR card was supposed to be signed, but for some reason the CPR instructor had stamped the card but not signed it. Frantically, I started reaching out to the CPR instructor so he could authorize my card over the telephone. All I needed was for him to say I had successfully completed the CPR course.

You would think that should be an easy fix, but the CPR instructor was in a meeting, so I had to wait for him to call the testing site when the meeting was over. My hands began to feel sweaty and those negative thoughts sparked in my brain again. My mind was telling me to go home and reschedule, but I would have had to wait two more weeks until I could retake the test.

After waiting a little over an hour, the CPR instructor finally called and confirmed that I completed the course at his location. Finally, I was able to take the test, which took no more than thirty minutes. My nervousness returned when it was time to learn the results. The instructor was happy to inform me that I had passed the exam with flying colors. I was so happy to reach the emotional achievement I had not felt since leaving the NFL.

The realization that I actually may be able to do well in this field was a momentum changer for my attitude and also a great mental boost to my confidence. Now the true test, of changing my body, was about to begin.

Chapter 15: I Am In My Own Way

My certification was now hanging on my bedroom wall next to my written goals. My self-image slowed down my desire to train new clients. I began to feel like I was back in football mode. Here I had studied and learned all the plays in the film room and now it was time for me to translate it onto the field. The problem was I was not in shape physically and mentally to execute the plays. There was no way I wanted to be a hypocrite, advising clients on how to eat healthy while I looked as though I didn't practice what I preached.

Deep down inside I knew what I needed to do, but I was procrastinating. The truth was that I was not mentally ready to make the big lifestyle change. After reading several self-help books, I began to learn some truths about myself. There were certain things I was doing that held me back from reaching my goals. The following areas, I realized, were subconsciously getting in my way.

Procrastination

Procrastinating is one of the ways we put off work or a new task. We also procrastinate if we've had a bad experience with the activity. We'd rather not face the task at hand because we think of the pain the task may bring into our lives. I'm sure I am not the only one that has said, "I am starting next week with my new diet" or "I will start exercising and eating right after my birthday." The thought of pain is weighing so heavily on our heart, we tend to delay our desires rather than attack them. Every time we delay our weight-loss journey we are giving ourselves a higher percentage to delay even longer because distractions are always going to come into play.

Think about the time you told yourself you'd start that diet on a Monday and then, out of nowhere, something comes up and you have to push your date back further. The opposite of delay is sense of urgency. Our journey for our weight loss can take a few months or a few years. We have to create that sense of urgency in our minds when we have a habit of delaying tasks that seem painful in our minds. Imagine if you had to go to prison and the warden told you that you couldn't get out of prison until you lose weight. I bet your sense of urgency would go through the roof. If you said to yourself, "I would surely take the weight off if that were the case," then why we don't have that sense of urgency now? What are we waiting for? You have full control of your body and mind but you must consistently train it to change your habit of delay.

Fear of Failure

During the journey of our weight loss we must see failure as a way of learning. We must experience loss to have new understanding. Think about how many times we all fell off our bikes when learning to ride. Our desire to learn how to ride a bike was so high that we understood falling was just part of the process. We understood that we would fall many times until we learned how to distribute our weight so the bike could be balanced upright. Falling on the ground hurt and sometimes left scars on our bodies. Our desire to learn how to ride a bike was so strong that we didn't mind the bumps and bruises. My question to you is—why does the process of losing weight have to be so different? During my weight-loss process I learned so much about my emotions, how different foods made my body react, different workouts I enjoyed or didn't enjoy, and even how to become a better cook.

My philosophy about failing is that it is part of the process of learning. Do not take it to heart that you are a failure; understand that you have learned what does not work. They say that Thomas Edison failed thousands of times before he learned the correct way to create the light bulb. Just think—if he had given up after a few, or even a hundred times, we might still be using fire to light up our houses. Your desire to win this weight-loss journey must be stronger than the fear of failing. It is okay to make mistakes. The key is to limit the same mistakes and learn from them. I preach to my clients that I don't expect them to be perfect through their weight-loss transformation, but I do expect them to become better with their choices. I can't tell you how many times I failed trying to cook a new recipe or stayed on the cardio machine the entire allotted time.

Instead of giving up and letting failure drive me away from my goals, I just made adjustments. Making adjustments is *key* when failing comes into play. I tell people I feel like I have a strong case of attention deficit disorder when I have to stay on the cardio machine for over twenty minutes. There are days I would envy people next to me who could ride the cardio machine for over forty-five minutes with no problem. Somehow, I knew I had to find a way to keep my butt on that machine. My strategy was to adjust my cardio routine by reading books, watching comedies on the Internet, and doing anything that was pleasurable to my mind. I now have no problem staying on the treadmill between thirty and forty-five minutes. Knowing that the treadmill was a major part of the process of losing my weight, I chose to adjust rather than quit.

Try to make adjustments with your plan so you can find better ways for you to complete each task. Successful people make adjustments when their initial chosen plan of action is not successful. If you do not like walking the treadmill, find other ways to enjoy your cardio. If you are tired of eating the one and only grilled chicken recipe you know how to cook, then simply adjust and find new ways to flavor your chicken.

Low Confidence

Having self-doubt in our hearts and minds will crush anyone's confidence. I am convinced that if you had to lose one pound to earn a million dollars, that task would be completed. Knowing this, we can agree that losing weight is not our real problem. The real problem we encounter is how to lose weight consistently. When I first started my weight-loss journey I doubted that I could drop below 300 pounds. Before earning my Personal Training certification my knowledge of how to lose weight was extremely limited. My ignorance explains why I attempted to starve myself to lose weight.

Starting your weight-loss journey with little or no knowledge on how to lose weight can be compared to a college student taking an exam without studying. The college kid will surely have a high level of self-doubt that he or she would be able to pass the exam. So how do we increase our level of confidence? We can slowly shut down our self-doubt by understanding and learning the craft of losing weight. I always ask the many people I come across, that try to lose weight and fail many times, "How many weight-loss books or articles have you read? "They look at me with a puzzled face and say, "Zero. "No one comes out his or her mother's womb knowing how to lose weight. People can either go to college to become a nutritionist and study how food affects our body or learn from a mentor that has been successful in achieving weight loss. You have chosen to learn from a mentor, which is why you are currently reading this book. The more you read about weight loss and understand how to successfully execute your plan, the more your belief will begin to increase.

Alienating Ourselves

Alienating ourselves from others is one of the worst things you can do when trying to lose weight. When we are not losing the weight that was expected, we seem to keep our emotions or disappointments to ourselves. We may have a feeling of embarrassment or feel no one will understand what we are going through. There were many times I was not seeing the results I wanted to see in the beginning and I would just keep my frustration to myself. I didn't feel that anyone would understand my pain and they would think I was a failure. I began to tell myself that I couldn't lose the weight and I was wasting my time.

I later talked to someone (who had success with their weight loss) about my struggles, and I gained so much hope after that conversation. Having a support system is a major factor during your weight-loss journey. Having someone in your corner to give you words of encouragement or teach you successful techniques can get you out of the rut. Look at many of the successful businessmen in the world and you will notice they all had mentors. Mentors are here to give advice during troubled times or to encourage you to keep working through adversity. I personally used self-help books to gain advice from people that could relate to my situation—many times the advice propelled me to reach new levels.

Journaling: What's Your Story?

Chapter 15: I Am In My Own Way

1. Do you procrastinate instead of attacking your fitness journey? ___Yes or ___No. Explain why.

2. What excuses have you used to put off your fitness journey? (Examples would be: not enough time, lack of motivation, or no one to work out with.) Share your story.

3. Do you fear failure? ____Yes or ___No. If yes, than explain why.

4. Does your lack of knowledge concerning exercise and nutrition cause you to procrastinate? ____Yes or ___No. Explain why.

5. How can you increase your level of expectation for your goals?

____
____
____
____

6. Do you have a mentor or coach to motivate and guide you? ____Yes or ____No. If yes, then share who that person is. If no, then explain why you don't have a mentor or coach.

____
____
____
____
____
____
____

Chapter 16: First Two Weeks On My New Journey

The first day of my journey I wanted to do what many successful people have done to keep a laser focus on their goals. As an athlete, I am a visual learner. So, I went to the nearest office supply store and purchased colorful printer paper. On those sheets I wrote down the type of person I wanted to become. From magazines I cut out pictures of successful businesspeople with very hectic schedules who still made time to exercise daily. The reason I chose this group is because I wanted to look at those men and say to myself, "*How is it that I cannot find time to exercise while these guys are far busier than I am, and they seem to make time for their exercise routine?*" These successful businessmen and women made adjustments, not excuses.

I taped up the colorful papers with phrases of who I wanted to become all over my bedroom, bathroom, and closet. My goal was to read them as I was getting dressed, brushing my teeth, or anytime I was in these rooms. I grabbed a flashcard and wrote the words, DON'T FEED YOUR FAST-FOOD EMOTIONS, so when I was driving I was reminded not to fall prey to my emotions. I taped the flash card to my steering wheel so the reminder would be clearly visible.

It may sound weird, but Bill Gates wrote down more than 10,000 of his goals on his walls to remind him why he must sacrifice and commit to his work. I woke up every day reading those papers on my walls to remind myself of who I wanted to become—until the concepts were permanently imprinted in my subconscious mind.

Our subconscious mind plays a movie in our head from all of our prior experiences we encountered. So, if you are like me and have produced experiences of failing or giving up, then your mind will also play those images for you. Reprogramming your subconscious mind takes time and constant practice in order to bring about change. Just as I had practiced for years failing to commit to my goals and eating the wrong foods time and time again, I had to learn to see myself as a different person over and over again.

Since I was accustomed to being coached and encouraged by coaches, I thought of a way to motivate myself with the technology of cell phones. I utilized my cell phone by making a two-minute video to remind me not to fall to the temptations of bad food. The video was a tool to encourage me to make the right choices when I wanted to fall back into my old habits. Think about if you had a fitness coach next to you every time you decided to make a bad choice. The fitness coach will surely motivate and encourage you to put that donut down. The video helped in the beginning (when I needed it the most) because it seemed like all the bad food and distractions were attacking me from every angle.

The beginning of my transformation was in the month of December. It was my hardest month ever because people love to eat around the holidays and I was surrounded by food. On the weekends, neighbors came over to hang out. They always brought bring dishes of food and desserts. Sometimes I'd have to retreat to my room because all that food looked so incredibly good; I felt my heart pounding very fast. In addition, my father loves to bake, and so he would bake new recipes every week. It was painful for me to look at his creations and not be able to eat any of them—it felt like torture. My best tactic to beat the temptation was to put the baked goods in a separate room so I wouldn't see them. I turned down many Christmas party invitations because I knew the urge to get off track would be devastating toward my attitude.

I tell people that when you are trying to get off drugs it's not good to visit the crack house frequently. Sometimes you have to make the best decision for your goal and stay away from the places that may cause you setbacks.

The most challenging part of my first two weeks was trying to eat every three hours. I'm the guy that never ate breakfast because I would rather get the extra sleep. I wouldn't have much of an appetite in the morning—since I was in such a rush to get to my destination. I was always trying to get every minute of sleep that was possible.

Cooking was not my favorite thing to do because I was not a good cook. As both a college and professional athlete, my meals were always prepared for me. I knew how to make basic sandwiches and hotdogs, but nothing about how to grill or bake food in the oven. I knew how to microwave but not sauté. This is why, in the past, I only ate salads and cereal in order to lose weight. Once I grew older and showed an interest, my mother began to teach me how to grill chicken and cook veggies so I would stick to healthy foods. The biggest problem I had was not having enough food available to eat. Sometimes I skipped meals, but that only created strong cravings, and I wanted to eat everything in sight. Even though I knew what to do to lose weight, staying disciplined to do it was challenging.

The numbers on my scale were not moving much those first two weeks, and my discipline was falling lower and lower every day. I beat myself up the next morning after eating a bad meal the previous day because I knew I should have done better. I told myself how stupid I was for eating the fast food instead of cooking my meals or making an excuse to not go to the gym because of being lazy. I even reached out to friends to jump on board with me so they could help motivate me. My friends did this for a few days and then eventually fell off the wagon. I blamed them for my lack of accountability instead of taking ownership of my own choices. I saw myself as a person that would do the right things when I had no choice. For example, I had no choice but to go to practice when playing sports, I had no choice but to make my weight limit during sports, and I had no choice but to get a job if I wanted to survive.

I battled with the realization of knowing that I was only as good as my options. I knew deep down inside I was better than that, and I needed to fix the problem right away. I searched for answers from personal development books, since I no longer had the luxury of sports coaching. I went to the nearest bookstore and bought several books on motivation. The understanding and knowledge I gained from these books changed my life forever. After reading several, I found the key to how successful people in the world become great. I learned how average people turn into bright stars. Sustaining inner motivation and excitement is essential to fighting through the ups and downs.

Journaling: What's Your Story?

Chapter 16: First Two Weeks on My New Journey

1. What is your hardest struggle when beginning your journey? (Check all that apply)

   □ Fast Food
   □ Finding the motivation to start workout regimen
   □ Lack of self-discipline to fight temptations
   □ Other______________________________________

   ____
   ____
   ____
   ____
   ____
   ____
   ____

2. What motivated you to start your journey?

   ____
   ____
   ____
   ____
   ____
   ____
   ____

Chapter 17: Change Happens And Is Sometimes Needed

It had been a month since starting my new fitness journey and my schedule changed completely. After receiving my personal training certification I was able to start my learning process. I went to the gym about 8a.m. and left close to 8 p.m. It was getting difficult to cook everyday as I had done in the past when I was at home all day. Coming home after doing a twelve-hour shift and then cooking for myself was the last thing on my mind. I noticed that I was skipping meals because of the lack of food I prepared.

My fast-food runs were increasing more and more by the week. I knew I had to come up with a solution for this new problem, but I didn't know what to do. Before I started working at the gym, exercise was fairly easy because I had all the time during the day to go to the gym myself. Now that I was working, it was hard to exercise before or after work. It seemed impossible to work out after 9 p.m. I was so used to doing it in the morning or anytime of the day I pleased.

I met some new friends at the gym and began to go out frequently with them every weekend. Unfortunately, I developed the bad habit of joining my friends at the Waffle House after the club let out. I ate like a pig at my favorite restaurants, only to wake up the next morning upset with myself because of my poor choices.

My good eating habits were falling apart, and the switch from being home all the time to having a social life affected my weight loss. I was having the time of my life, but I noticed my commitment to change for the best was being overshadowed. I came upon a crossroads between having fun with my new friends and making the right choices to lose my weight. The choice was only hard because it was a great feeling to be needed by others and spend fun time with them. My weight loss was at a standstill and my frustration with myself grew stronger and stronger by the week. I knew what I needed to do to lose weight, but I didn't know how to make the right choices day in and day out.

One day a trainer I was shadowing was talking to his client about meal preparation (prep). Never in my life had I heard of this term. I knew about leftovers, of course, but not meal prep. I learned that meal prep is a term used to cook a mass amount of foods at one time so you can have them available for the following days. The thought of warming up food that was two or three days old was disgusting. The trainer was teaching the client the concept of changing his routine first if he wanted to change the way he looked.

That advice stuck in my head all day, and I looked at my journey and saw the things I was not willing to change. I had made some positive modifications like not sleeping the whole morning, eating healthier meals, and sticking to my exercise regimens. Later that evening I pulled the trainer to the side and asked him about his technique of meal prepping. He said that meal prepping helped to keep one on track with a daily eating schedule. He told me that he cooked his food two or three times a week in a mass amount. He said he was too tired in the morning or after work to cook all the food he needed to consume daily. I told him that I was having a hard time eating meals every three hours. He led me to the trainer's break room and then pulled out a bag with several containers filled with food. He showed me his six-pack abs and said, "Remember, abs are made in the kitchen."

After work I rushed home and wrote down on piece of paper all of the things that I needed to change so I could become a completely new person. The first thing I wrote down was that I needed to try the meal prep technique. That same night I went to the store and bought Tupperware and large amounts of food. When I returned home I put on some music and started my meal prep process. I cooked turkey burgers, grilled chicken, grilled fish, sweet potatoes, scrambled eggs for breakfast, and vegetables. I stored all the food in the new Tupperware containers and placed them in the refrigerator. I was proud of my effort and told the whole world about my meal prep approach. The food looked great, but I was hoping it would taste as good as it looked three days from then.

Over the next few days I woke up in the morning, grabbed the Tupperware from the refrigerator, and placed it in the bag I took to work. After warming up the food in the microwave, I was quite surprised how good the food tasted. I guess the Tupperware seals in the taste and flavor better than a bowl covered with aluminum foil, which is how I did it in my old college days. The meal prep worked out great for my eating schedule. My daytime trips to the fast-food restaurants were cut down to zero, and I noticed the pounds dropping off. Meal prepping takes away a few hours of my Sundays, but not having to cook after work when I am tired from being on my feet all day is well worth it.

Changing my Environment

We all have heard the saying that we are a product of our environment. At that time of my life my environment was affecting my decisions with my weight-loss journey. I made some new friends from the gym and even more from my social activities. Going to bars, clubs, and other social events only seemed to hinder my success. You must remember that I had basically been housebound for close to a year after my NFL career ended. I looked forward to being around nice people and enjoying good music every weekend.

Many nights were spent drinking alcohol and then eating at fast-food spots, in order to absorb all the liquor. Did I order salads or wraps? Nope! I told myself that I needed to eat greasy foods to soak up the alcohol. This excuse made me feel better about my decision at the time when ordering my food but never felt good the next morning when I stepped on the scale.

I repeated this cycle almost every weekend. All my hard work during the week of exercising and eating well went right out the window. Monday through Thursday I was thoroughly following my eating and exercise plan—until the weekend approached. I had tracked my progress for the last four weeks and noticed I only lost four pounds. There needed to be a change because I worked too hard during the week to give it all away for a few nights of fun.

One Sunday I sat back and asked myself what I wanted more—to hit my weight-loss goals or continue to wreck my diet plan by partying on the weekends? Of course, the answer was my weight-loss goals, but I wasn't ready to give up the social life. I made a bet with myself to help me make the right decision—I could still go out, but only if I ate food listed in my food guide. I created a food guide with a list of lean meats, complex carbohydrates, fruits, veggies, and healthy fats. The bet was set in stone, and I was ready for my challenge for the upcoming weekend.

My buddies called me during the week and asked if I wanted to join them for a house party on Saturday. My plans were open, and I decided to take them up on the invitation. As usual, I followed my eating and exercise routines Monday through Friday, but we both know the real challenges appear on Saturday. Saturday finally arrived, and I knew I had to be strong with my discipline and make the right food choices. I ate my healthy dinner before leaving the house, so I would be sure to be full before arriving.

When I got to the party, you would have thought it was Thanksgiving, with all the food and desserts on the table. My eyes opened up wide like I was a kid staring at gifts under the

Christmas tree. I went straight to the bathroom and tried to get myself together. I looked at the mirror and said, "Terrance, you are stronger than that food, so keep it together." I walked out of the bathroom and one of my buddies immediately shoved an alcoholic drink in my hand and told me to enjoy. I started drinking and enjoying myself until the hunger pains started to come along. People around me were eating, and the food looked so damn good. I got up and walked around the food and dessert table, telling myself to sit back down. I then sat down again and continued to drink more alcohol.

An hour passed, my resolve tanked, and I grabbed a plate and piled on the food and desserts. The food tasted delicious and the desserts were amazing. I dove into that plate like it was my last meal on earth. I took my last bite and put the plate on the table. I sat back knowing I had just lost the bet, and I needed to make a change and make it fast. I stayed the rest of the night at the house party because I knew it would be my last one until I could show better discipline.

The next morning I woke up disgusted with myself and was scared to step on the scale. I made a promise to myself that I would not go out and be in an environment that may cause me to make bad decisions. We all know that distractions and peer pressure are hard to fight, especially if you are like me and hate to let people down. I also tend to fall into peer pressure because I am very competitive and don't like to look weak in front of anyone. I need to make the best decision for Terrance Pennington and no one else. Since I lost the bet, I had to make the decision to cut out my social activities until I increased my level of discipline.

Being a leader of your life means there will be times when you have to make the right decision for yourself, even if it disappoints others. That Sunday evening I called my buddies and told them that I would be cutting out my weekend partying because it was causing me to have setbacks. They all tried to convince me otherwise, but at the end of the day I knew that wasn't best for my goals.

Now that I had subtracted the social activities from my life, I wanted to replace them with something I enjoyed, so I would not have the feeling of missing out. The fear of missing out can affect us because we only have one life and we do not want to miss out on things that we may later regret. This lesson reminds me of the time I had to cut out my social life months before the NFL draft. My NFL agent sat me down and said, "Terrance, your friends and the fun will always be there. Take advantage of this opportunity to change your life and reach the ultimate goal. The next few months before the draft are very important, and you need to stay away from alcohol, drugs, and people that don't add value to you." It's funny to think that I was in the same predicament, and I knew I had to make the right decision for me.

Instead of going out on the weekends, I discovered Netflix and enjoyed staying home watching full-season episodes of television shows. I picked up other hobbies, such as playing miniature golf, bowling, and reading. These activities were fun, and they helped me to stay focused on my goals. I was happy with my weight-loss results every week and noticed my willpower strengthening. I suggest you look at your environment—your household, workplace, and friends. Ask yourself if the people you surround yourself with are helping you reach your goals or holding you back. You must make the right choice, now, that is the best fit for your goals. Your support system and real friends should be happy to help you reach your goals.

Journaling: What's Your Story?

Chapter 17:Change Happens and is Sometimes Needed

1. Do you follow a certain type of food guide? ___Yes or ___No. If yes, what type is it? Explain.
____
____
____
____
____
____
____

If no, please go to: www.TheTPexperience.com for helpful hints.

Chapter 18: Three Keys To Sustain Motivation

We all talk about what we want, but we never seem ready to go through the process. I am speaking from current and past experience in dealing with my weight loss. I kept promising myself over and over again, "*This time it's going to work.*" Or I thought, "*This time I am going to be very serious.*" I cannot count on my fingers how many times I said to myself, "*This week is my last week eating junk food,*" or "*I am going to start on Monday to get my act together.*" I wanted this attempt to be different this time.

What I came to realize was that everything I wanted was because of someone else's opinion of me. I wanted to lose weight so that no one would look at me funny when I took my shirt off. I wanted to lose weight so that girls would pay attention to me. I wanted to lose weight so my stomach did not hang over my belt for others to see. I wanted to lose weight to be healthier because my doctor said so. My reasons always had to do with the opinion of others and never for myself. If we are to be totally honest, most people have a strong desire to derive satisfaction from others. The point I am trying to drive home is to find out who you want to become.

I read and studied countless books of successful people—those that became successful in sports or business—those that have a dying desire to make a difference for themselves or to help others. This means they are not busting their tails day in and day out to make some girl proud of them. Bill Gates did not become successful because he wanted to earn enough money to show off for his friends. The feelings or emotions of your reasons to change for others are only so strong until the temptation of pleasure strikes—until that co-worker brings donuts to the office or your spouse takes you out to eat pizza. We all have been there, and then we go home upset or frustrated that we fell back into our old habits.

During my early years in sports, my motivation to follow the rules stemmed from not wanting to get punished by my coaches. It's the same with employees and their careers. They are motivated to show up to work on time when they are tired, sick, and dealing with bad weather, so they will not lose their job. The motivation is simply fear. When it comes to working out, we are used to being tired, sick, or citing bad weather as an excuse not to exercise. So, if instant fear has not been created, then we struggle with constant motivation.

People may say it takes twenty-one days to change a habit, but I believe instant fear changes a habit in a snap of a finger. If the doctor told you that eating one more cheeseburger would guarantee your death, I bet burger visits would immediately be crossed off your list. The problem is that we don't have instant fear, which can result in making the wrong choices.

You may be asking, "If we do not have those instant fears, then where does motivation come from?" To ultimately sustain your motivation you must know who you want to become, developing an increased level of expectation, and learning self-awareness of your emotions. Understanding and practicing these three phases will help keep your fire of motivation flaming at a high level. Motivation comes from within you. We are motivated by mental thoughts of pain or pleasure. Actions that bring emotions of pain are procrastination and making excuses for not starting or completing assigned tasks.

You may notice in your own life (and others)that it's not hard for us to make time to watch our favorite shows, go shopping for clothes, hang out with friends, or do any other activity that brings a feeling of pleasure. As you may agree with me, it may still not provide a solution of how to stay motivated through your fitness journey.

1. Who do you want to become?

When starting my fitness journey I never asked myself who I wanted to become when I reached my weight-loss goals. Being happy with how I looked in front of others was my only motivation. I taught myself and continue to teach others that in order to find true motivation, we must understand who we want to BECOME and believe we can become that person. The fear may push you to start, but it may not be enough to push you through the tough times of the weight-loss process.

You should often question your motivation. Ask yourself if you are on the quest to lose weight to satisfy other people's thoughts or opinions. Those thoughts are only strong if you absolutely fear others' opinions or destructive criticism. If you are a fairly confident person and you say you want to lose weight to look better, fear may not challenge you enough emotionally to press on through the hard times—like when you need to hit the gym at six in the morning on a snowy day. You must know what you want to become to make the change.

Thinking back on my college football career, I reflect upon the discussions amongst my locker room teammates about the possibility of playing in the NFL. We always talked about it, but I never truly felt I could be the one to actually play in the NFL. It was a wonderful thought, but that's all I saw it as—just a thought—until my coach made me believe that I could BECOME an NFL football player, once I put in the work. Instantly, my attitude changed once I knew, for sure, that I wanted to become an NFL athlete. So ask yourself who you want to become. This answer may come to you immediately or it may take a while. You may want to become a better example for your family to follow, or to become a more energetic person for your kids, or to become a more confident person.

Our subconscious mind tends to play movies that include all of our prior experiences. Reliving experiences of failing or giving up will automatically point our minds to self-doubt. Reprogramming your mind takes time and constant practice, but your mind will grow to change—just as we have practiced for years of failing to commit to our goals or practiced eating the wrong foods over and over again.

Over the years I had to, repeatedly, practice to see myself as a different person. This time, my reason to lose weight was to become someone I have never been. I wanted to become a more confident person so I could use that confidence to take advantage of opportunities in my life. I wanted to become a mentally tougher person and not give in to temptation or bad habits. I wanted to become a person that finishes a challenge and not makes excuses later. I wanted to become someone who enjoys a healthy-eating lifestyle. I wanted to become a demonstration for my family and others that watched me through my transformation.

When an athlete wants to become a champion, he must commit to the practices and habits it takes to become a champion. The passion to be a champion is so strong he or she is willing to go through the pain of being uncomfortable because being a champion is the greatest achievement. During the nine months of a mother's pregnancy she may grow a strong conviction that she wants to become a provider and protector for her child. When that baby arrives, the mother will wake up all hours throughout the night to check on that child. The mother will work two or three jobs if necessary to provide for her child. The mother will do anything she needs to by all means necessary because she has made a strong decision as to what she will become for the child.

2. Developing an increasing level of expectation

Developing an increasing level of expectation is having the confidence within you to complete the task. Our confidence plays a major factor in our attitude. It's the same confidence NFL-team players may have coming off a losing season the previous year and the head coach tells them that they can win the Super Bowl in the upcoming year. Every player wants to win but believing with full confidence is totally different. Having a high level of expectation is almost a feeling of guarantee. You may feel like I felt before achieving my weight-loss goal—that living in a new body feels like a dream that could never come to life. The feelings that come from having or losing guarantees makes the human mind change instantly.

You may be an employee that shows up to work every day, on time, and completes the duties your job requires for you to earn your paycheck. If your boss called you and told you that you might not get your check this week, I'm sure your attitude may change instantly and you may not care about going to work or completing your work on time.

Think about if you were a salesman and you were guaranteed that with every person you spoke to about your product guaranteed you a sale. I am sure you will bust your tail to get in front of as many people as possible. I was told the only thing in life that is guaranteed is death. I believe that a person's confidence is the greatest characteristic to strive for. Having enough confidence within is the deciding factor for someone to start their own business or go back to school to pursue a degree.

To be able to reach your goals it is a *must* to have a proven system to follow. Many people (including me) have started on the journey without a proven exercise or nutrition plan. Before starting your journey it is important to make sure your plan is a proven one. So, instead of attacking the task or seeing it as an opportunity to grow, we tend to delay it. We are afraid of failing, have self-doubt, or alienate ourselves because we think no one will understand our pain. Following a plan that includes guessing, hoping, and wishing will never provide high levels of expectations.

3. Controlling your state of mind

The strongest part of the body is the mind. Changing our state of mind is very challenging. The reason it is very difficult is because we are emotional creatures. We tend to act based on our emotions. Feelings of pain and pleasure may steer our actions. When we are doing something we enjoy, our state of mind is in the pleasure zone. When we are performing activities we dislike, we are in the pain zone. The key to mastering our state of mind when thinking about pain is to distract it with pleasure.

Many people practice this now by exercising while listening to music. Yes, the thought of exercising without music may feel dreadful. Music seems to put us in the pleasure zone mentally. The pleasure makes the exercise much more enjoyable. I use music to overshadow my thoughts of pain while I am cleaning the house, washing dishes, taking a shower in the morning when I am sleepy, or while in highway traffic.

Have you ever struggled to wake up in the morning to exercise but getting up at a similar time to catch a flight for vacation didn't seem as hard? The pain and pleasure thoughts will either motivate us or destroy our motivation. The secret to changing your state of mind is using visuals to spark up the brain and alter its state. For example, there were many times I would struggle to get out of my bed at 5 a.m. to exercise. I was mentally weak with my emotions when connecting with sleep. I remember many times hitting the snooze button and never getting up to make the workout.

One night I was watching the show, *The Biggest Loser*, and I suddenly realized that every time I viewed this particular show I became highly motivated. I sat back and thought about how I could use this feeling of motivation to my advantage. I adjusted my failing attempts to wake up in the morning and moved my cable DVR box into my bedroom. I decided to turn on an episode of *The Biggest Loser* when my alarm clock rang so I could transform my mental mind state from being lazy into being motivated. My "being tired" state slowly changed into excitement. I recommend you find something that brings you excitement when feeling unmotivated. Visuals can stimulate our brain and change our current feelings. It can be a part from a movie or motivational clip. Use the resources needed to change your mental state.

Being a visual person, I decided to write down on a flashcard a description of who I wanted to become. I kept this in my wallet. When I felt myself growing weak with temptations, I pulled out my flashcard and read it over and over again, until I became stronger. I also wrote these things on brightly colored paper and hung them up on my bedroom and bathroom walls. Above my bed on the ceiling I wrote, SLEEP IS THE ENEMY. I had a hard time waking up in the morning to workout at the gym. I knew I had to remind myself that the pleasure of sleep was not better than the pain of stepping on the scale weighing the same as the week before.

My emotions were always my downfall when trying to lose weight. If I was bored, I felt like eating. If I was sad, then I felt like eating. If I were eating healthily for a few days, I would feel like consuming a big cheeseburger because I missed the pleasurable taste. The common denominator was that my feelings were getting in the way of my goals. I knew I had to toughen up and control my emotions and urges.

During my times of playing football no one cared if I didn't feel like practicing. Coaches didn't care if I was sad because I was missing my family. No one cared about my feelings because they had to focus on winning games.

It is critical that you concentrate on your goals and not your emotions. Practice the techniques of changing your mental state so you can make the right choices. We may win and lose some battles, but the goal is to win the majority of the battles so we can ultimately win the war.

Journaling: What's Your Story?

Chapter: 18: Three Keys to Sustain Motivation

1. Who do you want to become?

____
____
____
____
____
____
____

2. To help guarantee your success—In what areas do you need the most help? (Check all that apply)
   □ Exercise routine
   □ Nutrition plan
   □ Coaching to keep me accountable
   □ Other__________________________

3. What actions will you take to control your emotions when experiencing moments when you don't feel like exercising or meal prepping?

____
____
____
____
____
____
____

Chapter 19: How I Created The Formula

There was no other way to arrive at the correct answer without discovering and implementing the proper formula. All throughout my years of playing sports I was told there was a formula for success. I knew I was never guaranteed a starter position when playing football. I was never guaranteed good grades just for showing up to class. The journey to lose weight is no different. I experienced it on my weight-loss journey, and I knew I had to follow a formula to succeed.

During my weight-loss journey I was following a process of what I thought was right or what was the least painful route. Instead of completing the full thirty minutes on the treadmill, I sometimes stopped at the twenty-minute mark. Instead of cooking my food for the next few days, I chose to buy food on the go as I went through my day. I chose to cut corners during the week and prayed when I stepped on the scale that I had done enough to lose a few pounds. My results went up and down because the formula I followed was inconsistent.

You may be a successful businessman or businesswoman that follows a formula to gain revenue and new customers. You may be a car mechanic and must follow a step-by-step formula to properly complete an oil change on a car. Their careers may be different, but the under-standing of following a formulated process to get the job done correctly is the same. I knew I had to create a formula to follow in order to reach my goals.

As I reflect, I can remember when I came up with this idea of the formula. It feels like it was only yesterday. I was home one Saturday morning, reading a sales book about how to become a great salesman. My purpose for reading the book was to become more like my boss. He was an awesome salesmen and he could sell salt to a snail. I asked him, "How can I learn to be a great salesmen like you?" He told me I needed to learn how to influence people and make them believe in my vision. He offered me a sales book and told me to start reading. The book explained that there is no salesman in the world that has the ability to close every sale. The salesman can only control his close ratio percentage with his sales formula. A good salesman will follow his natural ability to make the prospect like him, which can result in him making the sale. A great salesman follows a proven formula to close the sale. It's funny—at times, going through life, we can be in search of something and along the way we find a golden nugget to help us in other areas of our lives.

Shortly after reading the passage in the book and understanding what I was reading, it was easy for me to relate it to my weight-loss journey. I asked myself some very key questions—*Am I following a formula so I can hit my goals every week? Am I following a proven process? What established process have I followed consistently to create results?* I pondered for a few seconds and my brain immediately turned to football. I realized that during this weight-loss journey I was coaching myself.

During my years of playing professional football I played for some great coaches. The common denominator of all these coaches was their formula for success. One of my head coaches for the New York Giants preached to the team that the game is not won on Sundays. Instead, the game is won depending on how well we prepare and ***plan*** during the week—prepare the right game plan, plan to adopt the correct mindset to attack each day to get better, and plan for extra time to rehabilitate our battered bodies from injuries sustained from previous games.

In college, my offensive line coach, Bob Bostad, was a military-minded guy. Coach and I had many bouts about my lack of commitment to school and football during my earlier college years. He always pushed me past my limits, preaching to me that I would only reach my full potential once I decided to ***commit***—commit to practice, commit to film study, commit to weight lifting, and commit to school.

In high school my football Head Coach, Jimmy Sims, always lectured to the team that achieving **wins** built momentum and confidence. Correcting a mistake during film study was a win, making it on time to practice was a win, completing a great week of practice was a win, and scoring more points than our opponents was a win.

One of my funniest coaches for the Atlanta Falcons often spoke about ***repeating*** success. He wanted us to understand that in order for us to repeat the good habits that helped us to win, we must also understand how to repeat our successful routine. I wrote those words down on a piece of paper and read them to myself over and over again. I created my formula to succeed and put it into action.

Plan-Commit-Win-Repeat is a formula that I followed to lose over one-hundred pounds, and it has helped many others I have coached to hit their goals. Each part of the formula has its own purpose and so we must consistently follow the formula.

Chapter 20: Plan

My mother was a great planner, and it would drive me nuts at times when I was a youngster living at home. She wrote out the plan on how to correctly clean the house to her standards. When I was attending private schools my mother made me set aside time each Sunday to iron all my uniforms for the whole week. My mother would plan events to ensure we arrived on time. One thing I can say about my mother—is that we were never late for an event.

As we become adults and get a job, we are forced to plan for work. Think about how much planning we do when it revolves around our career. We plan on how much more sleep we can get before we have to wake up to get ready for work. We plan on what time we must leave the house to make it to work on time. We plan personal activities outside our work schedule such as vacations, our children's events, and the time it takes to grab lunch and make it back to clock in on time. So why do we plan so well for work but not for our weight-loss journey? Is it because our job superiors inform us of our work schedules a week or weeks in advance? This, in turn, allows us zero-to-little tolerance when giving excuses for arriving late or missing work.

For those of you who have never held a job before and cannot relate to my example, think about being in high school and understanding the importance of being on time for class or sports activities. Every person has been through school and remembers the short ten minutes allocated in between classes to get books from the locker, talk with friends, or possibly grab a snack from the vending machines. How about the athletes in high school that had to plan enough time to talk with friends, grab a bite to eat, and get dressed all in thirty minutes before practice started? When trying to reach your fitness goals, planning is vital. It took me months to truly understand this concept.

Planning for nutrition and exercise

During the first few months of my weight-loss journey, I did not plan the time to cook food on Sunday so I could have healthy food options for the upcoming days. When I didn't have my food prepared, I would normally eat fast food or skip meals entirely. During the week I made attempts to exercise at least five days a week, but I often fell short and exercised only three or four days. I would miss my workout days because I allowed other plans to get in the way. Isn't it funny that we will miss our workouts days but we will never miss work itself? We guard our work times and make sure no one or nothing gets in the way.

There was one day when I planned to exercise in the evening and I received a phone call from a friend asking for a ride to the airport. Of course, I agreed to take him to the airport and after coming back my energy and excitement for exercising went away. I went home and sat on the couch and started relaxing as though I never did have any plans to exercise.

What if the same friend requested a ride while I was on my way to work? I'm sure my answer would have been "no" and hoped he understood that my job was important for me to keep. I am definitely not saying that you should tell your friends "no" when they are in need of help when you are on your way to work. I want you to think about how much we guard or protect the things that are important to us or when we are held accountable. We protect the time we plan to watch our favorite TV shows, we protect family vacation times, and we guard the time we spend playing video games and taking part in other recreational activities.

The good news is we know how to plan and we practice it daily. My excuse for poor planning was that there was never enough time in the day. My work day started around 8a.m. at the gym and I didn't return home until 8 p.m. I came home so tired and physically drained. The television and couch were the only things on my mind once I entered the house. My feet hurt from standing up all day, and all I wanted to do was lie down. My mind was telling me to go in the kitchen and cook my food needed for the next day. My body was telling me to enjoy this relaxation time on the couch. Almost always my body won the fight. My planning process was terrible, which led to terrible results. I had to make a decision to change my process and have my food ready for the next day. I also had to make a commitment to complete my exercises for the week. If you are in this similar boat, then follow this planning process.

One of the best decisions I made was to start planning out my week on Sundays so I could thoroughly follow my nutrition and workout plans. In my room I put up a dry erase board and drew a line through the middle of it. The left side represented my exercise schedule and the right side of the board represented my nutrition. I wrote out the times I would exercise under each day. Since I planned the time, I made sure I encountered no distractions during those exercise routines.

As I continued to learn more about myself, I realized that exercising before work was best for me because I had fewer distractions. In the beginning, waking up early in the morning to do this brought forth feelings of pain. Maybe you feel the same way? I practiced and trained my mind to think that working out in the morning was needed, because exercising after work wasn't consistent. I could guarantee exercising in the morning, but I could not guarantee doing so in the evening due to my hectic work schedule. If, for some reason, I missed a day during the week, I made sure I planned to make up the exercise day during the weekend.

On the right side of the board I wrote out the days I would cook my food for the whole week. I often chose Sundays and Wednesdays for meal prep since my workloads at the gym were lighter on those days. Sometimes my days would switch because of events I may have planned on those days. Planning actually made life easier to stay on track. In the beginning, it seemed harder or time consuming because I had bad experiences with my mother, but in the long run it saved me so much time and so many mistakes.

I've coached many people who tell me that they don't have time to make it to the gym or do not have enough time to cook their food. Another challenge my clients struggle with is fitting in the time to exercise because they work forty to fifty hours a week. Everyone has heard before that we all get the same number of hours each day. My old coach often told the team the difference from an average player and great player was how they managed their time. You may feel there is not enough time in the week to fit in your exercises and prepare your meals.

When I mentor clients, I break down the hours we are given every week and figure out how they are spending their time. My question to you is, how do you use your time? So let's break down the hours we are given weekly and figure out where we can find time to hit your goals. There are 168 hours in a seven-day week. If we work eight hours a day in a five-day work week and sleep eight hours a night for seven days, then that will equal ninety-six hours being used to function and support ourselves. We may spend forty hours a week with leisure activities such as social media, television, family time, and talking on the phone. We now have thirty-two hours remaining for the week that we can use to exercise and meal prep food.

I know there are some individuals who still may say they don't have time to reach their goals. I teach my clients how to substitute time. I figured out if I was going to wake up energized early in the morning to exercise, then I couldn't stay up late watching my favorite television shows. I chose to go to sleep earlier in order to wake up earlier. If you have to wake up an hour earlier to exercise, then do it. If you have to exercise late at night after school or work, then do it. When you have a desire to win, or hit your goals, then you must commit to whatever it takes to make sure you reach your goal.

Planning for change of schedules

One of the most common reasons people give up is because of changes in schedules. Schedules can often alter our lives—our own work schedule, our kid's sports schedules, our spouse's schedules, and school schedules. We cannot control all schedule changes. Humans are creatures of habit, and when we are forced out of our habit, we can mentally breakdown. So many times during my weight-loss journey my work schedule interfered with my exercise routine. Being a personal trainer, I had to train clients in the morning and evening. It's my duty to work around the client's schedule. I would be lying if I said it didn't bother me because I formed a comfortable habit with my routine. Feelings of frustration, anger, and stress would suddenly run through my body when I had to change my routine.

I often battled with these strong feelings until I read a book that changed my perspective. Mark Patterson's book, *In the Pit With a Lion on a Snowy Day.*[*] This book helped me understand that when you are in a pit there is nowhere to run, so you have to face the lion. Fighting against the lion on a snowy day would be a disadvantage because we do not have the paws and claws to sustain our balance on a snowy and slippery surface.

When you are faced with your fitness challenge, the circumstances may often change. Your situation may start out favored but then change in a split second and throw you off your game. We must make two choices when something out of our control comes up and changes our schedule. The first choice is finding a way to dig deep and fight through the adversity regardless of how challenging it may be. The second choice is to throw in the towel because you are not willing to find a way to win through the storm. When your schedule changes you must go back to the drawing board and find out a way to win. Every time my schedule changed I erased my current schedule and planned a new one. Remember, our initial goal in the beginning is to lose weight and enjoy how we look or feel. Our initial goal is not to lose weight with the perfect schedule that never changes. Always go back to your initial goal to help you cross the finish line.

[*]Mark Patterson, *In the Pit With a Lion on a Snowy Day* (Multnomah Books; First edition, 2006).

On your journey you must become a marathon runner, not a sprinter. During the marathon, a runner may have to change the running pace or change the plan in figuring out how to pass an opponent who is blocking the inside lane. The marathon runner has to develop mental and physical endurance to finish the race. The runner must also develop patience during the race because he or she understands it's not a short race. Change your mindset to become the long-distance runner and not the one-hundred meter sprinter.

Journaling: What's Your Story?

Chapter 20:Plan

1. Do you schedule your exercise days in advance? ___Yes or ___No. If not, explain why.

2. Do you meal prep? ____Yes or ____No. If not, then explain why.

3. What will you change to create time for your goals?

Note: For meal prep guidance go to: www.TheTPexperience.com

Chapter 21: Commit

The second part of the formula is committing to the plan. Webster's dictionary[*] defines the word "commit" as to pledge or carry into action. There is a difference between wanting to lose weight and having the desire to lose weight. In the beginning of my weight-loss journey I wanted to lose weight and never understood I needed to have a desire instead. As you read from my early childhood and up to my college days, I always cut corners. I would do the minimum just to get by. So, of course, I took the same approach to losing weight. I knew I was supposed to eat healthy all the time, but I chose to do it only some of the time. I knew it was best to eat four to five meals a day, but I chose to eat only two or three times a day. I knew I needed to exercise regularly, but I chose to do it when I felt like it. I tried to cheat the process to lose weight but the scale always told on me.

Every time I committed to the plan and drew on my board, I never missed a step and I received great weight-loss results. My scale went up and down the first few weeks of my journey. This yo-yoing often frustrated me, but I knew it was my fault. It was my fault I ate the donut, my fault I didn't go to the gym, and my fault that I skipped meals. The question I had to ask myself was why I still continued to make decisions I knew would not help me reach my goals. You've heard the old saying, "I want to have my cake and eat it too." I chose to eat the food that made me start my weight-loss journey instead of eating the foods that would end my weight-loss journey.

So many others I mentor now often say they have trouble committing. They think they cannot commit to their workout plan or eating plan. I ask them how they committed to their two-year plan with their phone provider. I also asked them a couple more questions. How did you commit to paying your mortgage every month for the next thirty years? How did you commit to going to work every day, every week, every month, and every year?

The common denominator of all these commitments is the choices we are given. You are given the choice to either make the payment or encounter no service for your cell phone. Make the payment or receive an eviction notice on your front door. Go to work or get fired. It's sad to say, but most of us are better when we have no choice. In the United States we operate under a

[*] Source: www.merriam-webster.com

democratic government and we are given rights and choices. Other countries and government systems do not offer their citizens choices because they believe they can make better decisions for them.

If you disagree with me, then let me present this to you. Imagine that you are thrown into solitary confinement in prison. The judge states that you are mandated to stay in the prison for the rest of your life until you reach your weight-loss goal. How do you think you will approach your weight-loss journey? I am sure you will do whatever it takes to lose your weight quickly to become free again.

So my question to you is: Do you need to have fewer decisions so you can have a better chance at success? I was in denial of this concept until I was aware that desserts were my drug. If anyone knows me well, they understand how desserts are my biggest weakness.

In the biblical story of Adam and Eve, I understand why Eve took a bite of the apple. I judge no man or woman when they battle strongholds. Any dessert with cream cheese icing or vanilla icing will tear down all the walls of my discipline powers. Some people struggle with carbs, like bread. I know for sure my wife is addicted to the queso cheese you order from any Mexican restaurant.

What is your stronghold that you know is like a drug you cannot say no to? It may be friends, food, environment, or your intimate relationships. You may be confused when I mention an intimate relationship. The client's spouse, at times, becomes a distraction for the client. The husband may come home with a pizza and distracts my client from choosing healthier meal options. Another case is where the wife wants to take my client out on a dinner date to her favorite restaurant. When committing to a goal, your partner's bad influences can become challenging.

The activities are counterproductive to each other's goals and desires. If your spouse is not on the same page, and the influence is pushing you further away from your goals, then a change needs to occur. Your spouse has the right to eat the way they choose, but I do believe your spouse should always try to add value to your life. Your spouse should help you to reach your goals and not hinder you with their influences. It might sound bad, but when I coach clients that are single, I am ecstatic. This delighted feeling I get is not because they have yet to find their intimate partner. The main reason is because it's hard to tell the person you love the word "no."

Telling women I dated during my weight-loss journey the word “no” when they asked me to take them out to eat was difficult. Telling them “no” when they wanted to order pizza was hard too.

If you have this difficult situation on your hands, I recommend you talk to your partner about your needs. Tell your partner that his or her influences are not helping you to reach your weight-loss goals. Express to your partner that you know they care about your happiness, and it would make you happy if they would not influence you to partake in activities that may derail you from your commitment to lose weight. Tell your partner that you are not asking them to change their ways, but that it would be helpful not to entice you with food or things that you may be very weak against. Hopefully, your partner will understand and make the decision to help you on your mission.

Executing this type of communication helped me with my relationships, but it was not the answer to my dessert problem. My dessert addiction was serious, and it didn’t matter how much I knew it was bad for my diet, I still wanted every piece of it. Many late nights I woke up, strolled into the kitchen, and looked longingly at the desserts that were calling my name. I knew I should not take even one bite, but I would say things to myself to make me feel better about my bad decision. “Well, I will do an extra ten minutes on the cardio machine,” or “these little bites will not hurt.” The little bite would turn into bigger bites and I later noticed that I ate the whole dessert. So, I took the same approach that drug addicts and alcoholics use to end their addictions. I made sure I was never around sweets. I did everything I could not to have any desserts in my house.

Legendary comedian Chris Rock said on one of his standup comedy shows, “Men are as faithful as their options.” I am not saying that this is true for all men, but I knew it was true for me and my dessert options. Once I made up my mind how I would get over this stronghold of desserts, I went into my kitchen and threw all my cream-cheese-filled desserts in the trash can. Throwing away the desserts made me think of a woman throwing away her favorite pair of shoes. Desserts and I had good times together, but the good times had to finally end. This practice worked for me because I had no choice but to skip desserts. If I chose to eat desserts and reward myself, I decided to eat them at restaurants and never take the leftovers home.

Commitment is not just about following the rules or a proven process. It takes commitment to acknowledge your strongholds and keep them out of your environment. Today, as I am talking to you as a fitness expert, I still see dessert as my drug of choice. When I am following a strict meal plan, I often ask my wife to hide any desserts she may purchase from the store. Another technique I use when trying to withstand strongholds is to write down the words "discipline" and "integrity" on my hand.

The holidays were the hardest times for me to stick to my eating plan. From Thanksgiving to New Year's, cakes and pies always seemed to be right there in front of me. I often was invited to house parties, ball events, and social functions that consisted of many desserts. Writing the word "discipline" on my hand and reading it during the events helped me to stay focused. I am often reminded about my goals and what it takes to reach them. It takes discipline and keeping my integrity to hit these goals. I have had a few people ask me why those words are written on the back of my hand. Once I share with them the purpose, they often agree and decide to implement the strategy for themselves.

Saying you are going to do something and actually doing it are two totally different things. Yes, others may look at my hand and think I am weird, but one thing I do know is that I am successful at the end of the night—successful by keeping my integrity and the discipline needed to keep my commitment. Many people may laugh, but being committed to my goals and the process is more important than being in denial of my strongholds.

Integrity through commitment

One of my mentors, Renee Bobb, shared with me that the secret to being successful is doing what you said you were going to do. It's important to keep your integrity at a high standard when dealing with business, relationships, and surely yourself. We all can tell lies to others, but we cannot lie to ourselves. We can tell others the reasons why we are not losing weight. We can blame thyroid hormones, but we've never been diagnosed for thyroid problems. Another excuse could be that we are big boned. I have even heard a client tell me they cannot lose weight because it's hard for women to do so. The real answer we cannot lose weight is because we cannot commit to the process of including efficient nutrition and exercise in our lives.

I have told myself lies to feel better about my poor decisions—I can't start my weight-loss mission until after my birthday, or I cannot begin to lose weight until the start of the New

Year. I told myself anything and everything under the sun so I could feel better about my self-image. Once we make our decision, then we must commit with full force.

Recently I was coaching a young lady who always talked about how she was frequently frustrated with her weight-loss results. She would spend the last few days of the year mentally preparing mentally to start her weight-loss journey—one of her New Year's resolutions. She would buy a gym membership and nice gym outfits. She will announce to the world that she is going to lose the same fifty pounds she has been attempting to lose for the past ten years. Her friends and coworkers are now watching her to see if she is going to lose the weight or make another failing attempt.

The New Year arrives and she is ready for another shot at hitting her goals. The first week her momentum and excitement is at a high level. On week two she begins to make excuses for her lack of commitment. Either she is tired from work or makes other plans during the time of her exercise schedule. As the weeks go by, she goes to the gym less and less. The good eating habits starts to die out and she is back to eating fast food.

After a month she begins to lie to her girlfriends, saying she is consistently going to the gym and eating well every day. The pressure is on her shoulders, and lying about her routine to her friends only makes her feel worse about her efforts. In the beginning she was bragging about her weight-loss journey, and now she changes the subject when friends bring up the topic.

Your story may not be exactly the same, but maybe you have not followed through with your commitments. Once you start down this road of destroying your integrity, you lose confidence in yourself. Always remember your actions must become congruent with your words. Show people your actions, not just your words. Prove to yourself that you will follow through by all means necessary. Most of all, prove to yourself that your health and integrity are most important.

So many people often say their health is priceless and worth all the money in the world. If you have the same beliefs about your health, then why not apply this approach to your weight-loss journey—like it is your billion dollar company? You are the CEO and you make all the decisions for your company. As the CEO of your body you must take full responsibility for all decisions and promises. It is now time to change your past failing experiences and focus on keeping your integrity. It's time to stand up for what you know is the best decision for your life.

We all know the outcome if we do not commit or give it our all. We have arrived at that outcome so many times in our lives.

The more important question is, “What might happen if you give it your all for thirty days straight?” You may not know because you may have never given it your all before. When I say “give it your all,” I want you to turn yourself into a thoroughbred horse. Have you ever seen a cowboy jump on his thoroughbred horse and give the horse the command to go? What you probably never witnessed is the horse turning around and asking the cowboy, “How fast and far do I need to go?” The horse runs full throttle ahead when he is tapped on the rear with the whip. Cowboys also put blinders on the horse because they do not want the horse to become distracted by their surroundings. God has given you the body that has the ability to give an all-out effort, but it is your job to develop the thoroughbred-horse mentality. Understand that committing is the only way you will ever hit your goals in your journey.

Journaling: What's Your Story?

Chapter 21: Commit

1. What things are you currently committed to in your life? (Examples could include: family, job, career, business, or spirituality.)

2. What actions are you going to start taking to increase your commitment level?

Chapter 22: Win

Practicing your willpower to make the right decision day in and day out is a trained process. Climbing into your car and immediately putting on your seat belt is an example of past training. We did not come into this world knowing that attaching our seat belt is the first action taken before starting our vehicle. We were taught the importance of seat-belt protection and so we practiced this action every time we entered a vehicle. You are not forced in any way to put on your seat belt. The law requires you wear it and if you get caught, you may be penalized.

The concept of winning today in our society refers to your end result. So much pressure is put on us to win at the end of the battle, and we don't focus on the wins that are needed during the battle. At the end of the day you can perform the winning choice or the losing choice.

The sport of football is a team sport, and there are three important phases. These three phases are offense, defense, and special teams. Each phase has its own purpose for the team to win the game. There were NFL games I played in where we would be trailing the game through the first three quarters. Our offense was playing like trash and we could not win enough plays to keep the drive going. Our defense made enough winning plays to keep our opposing offense from scoring touchdowns as well. We were grateful for the defense winning more plays than the opposing offense. Without our defense we would, for sure, have been behind by much more than three points. In the fourth quarter, we knew, as the offense, it was time to put a good drive together. We came out of the huddle ready to score and win the game. The first three plays were successful and we gained momentum. The streak of winning plays instantly changed our attitude, and we played harder and longer than our opponents. Yes, there were plays during our last drive that were not successful, but because we built up so much belief we went onto the next play like they never happened. Our offense ended up scoring a touchdown with no time remaining on the clock, and we won the game.

The moral of this story is that we had to make enough winning plays to win the battle. The consistent wins can build your belief and consistent losses can diminish your belief. At the end of the battle our wins must outweigh our losses. Please understand that you are not perfect and you will make mistakes. The best athletes in the world who train all day and every day make mistakes. The important key to understand is we are in full control of our decisions and our attitudes. Your decisions will either make you feel good or bad. They will get you closer or further away from your goals. You will have setbacks and make wrong decisions.

During my weight-loss journey I viewed my decisions as wins and losses. If I chose to eat a slice of pizza, that was a loss. If I woke up on time to go to the gym and exercise before work, it counted as a win. When I meal prepped on Sunday, that was a win. I was fully aware of my attitude after I completed the winning decision and also of my attitude after I completed a losing decision. If you've ever played sports before, think about how great the teams felt when rolling on a three-game winning streak. Then think about your team attitude when experiencing a three-game losing streak. I'm sure practice sucked when you were on a losing streak.

For those of you who have never played sports but still follow them, I am sure you have noticed there are teams in different sports that are always in the run for the championship title. Year after year they are the last few teams standing for a chance to win it all—teams such as the San Antonio Spurs, the New England Patriots, and the Boston Red Sox. What these teams have in common is their winning culture. They preach to their athletes about playing their sport the right way. They demand that their athletes approach every practice, film study, opportunity, and experience with a winning mentality.

Look at your meals, exercises, and choices and ask yourself if you are, in fact, approaching them with a winning mentality. Are you settling for mediocre choices and effort? I know I was settling at times and not approaching every opportunity with a winning mentality. My method changed once I was aware of my attitude after my wins or losses. After a good week of eating and exercising I would step on the scale and notice I dropped a few pounds. The win for the week motivated me to go to the store on Sunday to buy my food for the next week. After a bad week of eating and exercising, I would step on the scale and notice I gained a few pounds. The loss encouraged me to run to any fast-food place to drown out my sorrows—by eating a juicy cheeseburger and large order of fries.

These practices would only change once I adjusted my losing decisions. One Saturday after experiencing another losing week, I sat back on the couch to come up with a plan to fix my problem. Instead of focusing on seven days of making the right choices, I focused on one day of making the right choices. I wrote on my dry erase board and created a checklist for things I needed to execute on any given day.

The list would be different at times because certain days I would cook or exercise. Some of my rules were to eat five small meals a day, drink a gallon of water, meal prep, and then wake up in the morning to exercise. These checklists kept me accountable on a daily basis, so when I stepped on the scale I could measure my week and look at the areas where I needed to improve.

There were weeks I had a perfect track record and there were weeks when I made a few mistakes. The ultimate goal for the use of my chart was to improve daily and weekly. The checklist also raised my excitement level to continue to win with my good choices since I was on a great winning streak.

You may have been told it takes twenty-one days to build a habit. I often tell my clients that it is the type of day they are having that builds the habit. Experiencing twenty-one days with the majority of the days ending as losing days will never change the habit. You will never experience the highs from the change and also never experience the benefits of the change. Your twenty-one days must have more wins than losses and must have a streak of wins somewhere during the time span.

If you are exercising more and still experiencing more losses than wins, it's time to evaluate your week. Do you have a great winning streak Monday through Thursday? Does your winning streak end when the weekend approaches? If so, then focus on building winning streaks for the weekends and follow your checklist. Notice what choices are holding you back. I recommend you try this technique if you see yourself losing motivation. This practice will also keep you accountable of your daily choices. Remember that our choices determine our outcome. Focus on your choice to win daily and you will create a win for the week. Focus on winning four consecutive weeks and you create a win for the month.

Journaling: What's Your Story?

Chapter 22: Win

1. How will you begin to make winning choices?

   ____
   ____
   ____
   ____
   ____
   ____
   ____

2. In what areas do you need to develop winning streaks to increase your results? (Circle or fill in.)
   - □ Weekend nutrition decisions
   - □ Exercise consistency
   - □ Eating breakfast consistently
   - □ Other______________________

Chapter 23: Repeat

Years ago I read a survey asking the top one-hundred richest people in America what was the one thing they needed to become successful. Many threw out answers such as work ethic, integrity, willpower, and other qualities that were all important. The majority of them said it took focus to become successful. Think about the salesman that bangs out the phone calls to his prospects day after day to generate sales. Think about the hall of fame athletes that practice the fundamentals day in and day out year round to become the greatest. Think about the mother that sits with her child every night making sure the child's homework is complete. Now think about the salesman that is inconsistent with his phone calls. What is the outcome of the athlete that chooses to skip the fundamentals some days during practice? How successful is the mother that inconsistently holds the child accountable for doing his or her own homework? Repeating the process to win is a practice of willpower.

The last step of the formula is by far the hardest step to follow on your fitness journey. This step separates you from either reaching or quitting your goals. This step determines whether your fitness journey will take six months or six years. In Webster's dictionary* the word "repeat" means to make, do, or perform again. Starting the fitness journey is the easy part, but finishing the journey is the best part. When starting your fitness journey you are excited and motivated to make your changes. The gym membership is purchased, we tell everyone on Facebook or at work, and we go shopping to buy the food needed to make the nutritional changes. As we go along our journey we are sidetracked by distractions or unsatisfactory results.

When I meet with a new client to life coach or train them, I often ask them this question: "If we made a bet for one thousand dollars for you to lose only one pound, would you take the bet?" They pause for a second, thinking this is a trick question and soon reply "yes" with a huge smile. The next question I ask is, "Then why can't you lose one pound thirty times or as many times as needed to reach your fitness goals?" All of them make the same puzzled face and respond by saying, "I don't know why I can't."

The reason why it feels impossible is because keeping our focus to repeat the same activity every day or every week is really tough. It is tougher now than ever before because there

*Source: www.merriam-webster.com

are so many distractions that can take over our focus. We can easily become distracted by friends, kids, social media, stress, work, schedule changes, food, events, and spouses. As you know, the list goes on and on. It takes a strong desire and obsession to be able to repeat your process over and over again. The truth is that our journey is not an overnight one, and it will take steady focus and drive to reach the end of the tunnel.

This step was very difficult for me during my weight-loss journey. I could repeat the process of going to work every day or watching the same television show every week. My successful process was eating every three hours, working out consistently, saying no to desserts, drinking a gallon of water, and meal prepping every Sunday. It was my responsibility to repeat this process over and over again until I got results.

At this point you may be asking yourself exactly how I learned how to repeat the process to lose over one-hundred pounds. I believe I developed a slightly obsessive compulsive disorder (OCD) following the first three steps of my formula. Some may call it a disorder, but it helped keep order in my life. I made sure that planning, committing, and winning were a must. There was no other way for me to become satisfied with my day.

Are you obsessed with something that must be done a particular kind of way? My wife's OCD is about seasonings and how each label must be facing the front of the cabinet. When we first met I often joked about it; I would play games with her and turn the seasoning bottles the opposite way. She would panic and lose her mind when she saw the labels facing the wrong way.

The funny thing is that I am the same way with my meal prep, exercise, and other things that help me to stay healthy. If I don't eat my meals on time, I get upset. If I do not go to the gym and exercise at least one time during the week, I feel myself getting cranky. I remember, at times, that my mother became upset because I brought my own healthy food to her house to eat instead of eating the food she cooked.

Please don't get me wrong and think I am recommending that you become over compulsive in your weight-loss journey. I am simply saying that you must create an obsession or strong desire to follow your plan and execute it every day. Of course, there will be times you make bad eating decision or miss a few days of working out. Once you get upset (because you know you hold yourself to a high standard), then that is when you know your desire to lose weight is growing. You must hold yourself to a high standard because it takes a high level of productivity to get to your goal.

So many of my previous clients either executed only half of their workout or ate only two meals a day instead of eating every three hours. Then they would say to me, "Well at least I've done something." Have you made this statement before? I know I have said this to myself when I started my weight-loss journey.

Imagine you are an owner of a company. Of course, you hold high standards for your employees and yourself. One of your employees comes in an hour late and his response to you is, "At least I made it in today." I am sure, as the owner, you will not find that comment to be acceptable. Imagine you are a teacher and one of your students turns in a five-page research paper. You have stated to the class and wrote on the syllabus that the paper must be at least ten pages long. He hands you the paper and responds with, "At least I've done something." If we don't accept those standards from others, then why should we accept those standards for ourselves?

The secret to getting to your fitness goals relies on the strength of your will and determination to repeat the process it takes to win. You need to repeat the process of getting back on the treadmill after being on it the past four weeks. You must repeat the process of waking up in the morning to go to the gym even though it's raining outside. The process is part of the grind, and we must repeat the grind over and over again. Remember, we repeated the process to eat the unhealthy food and lay on the couch day in and day out. We also repeated the process of constantly giving up. This time with your attempt to reach your goals, you will make this journey your desire and train yourself to become in love with the formula—the formula to plan, commit, win, and repeat is your playbook to win every day, week, and month!

Journaling: What's Your Story?

Chapter 23: Repeat

1. Why is it hard for you to keep your focus and repeat your plan?

2. If you notice your focus is declining, what will you do to get back on track?

Chapter 24: How To Become Great at Weight Loss

To become "great" at anything, you must overcome your weaknesses. You will only reach new levels of success once you minimize the weaknesses that are holding you back. In the beginning of my journey, my weaknesses were committing to my plan, completing a full workout, cooking a variety of foods, waking up early in the morning, and sticking to my eating regimen on the weekends. Those weaknesses always landed me with average results. When all is said and done, if you want to become a new and confident person, you first need to be great at losing weight. It is so hard to be great at something if you have weaknesses slowing your progress.

I mentor a young kid by the name of Charles who aspires to become a successful basketball player. He is great at shooting, ball handling, and passing. His coaches are always preaching to him that he needs to be better in his defensive skills, rebounding, and left-hand layups. Charles enjoys practicing his basketball skills daily, weekly, and monthly. What is slowing him down on his road to greatness, however, is the fact that he is only playing to his current strengths. He practices more on these particular skills because he enjoys the outcome. He loves seeing the ball going through the net, and he enjoys making the perfect pass and hearing his friends tell him that he did a fantastic job. Lastly, he enjoys showing off his ball-handling skills in front of his teammates. Charles chooses to spend the least amount of time on the things that are stopping him from reaching that next level of greatness.

Charles needs to understand that he will only reach the next level once he changes his focus—to spend more time improving upon his weaknesses by utilizing defensive play, rebounding, and left-hand layups. The reason why Charles shies away from tackling his weaknesses is because he does not enjoy the feeling of pain or failure. Charles experiences pain when he does not make a layup, get the rebound, or make a great defensive play. He experiences failure more times than success in the beginning stages of improving upon his weaknesses. Charles also needs to realize that it is okay to go through the pain and failure in the beginning, because the more he challenges those weaknesses the better he will become. As Charles does this, feelings of pain and failure will turn into feelings of joy and success. Charles' situation is no different than yours or mine.

So many times people tell me that they want to make getting healthy a lifestyle change. I often tell them, "For this to be a lifestyle change, you have to enjoy the lifestyle." To accomplish this you need to be diligently practicing the lifestyle you want each and every day. If you want to eat healthy all the time, then you need to enjoy eating healthy foods. If you want to include exercise in your weekly routine, then you must like working out. The reason why we do not enjoy this type of lifestyle is because we do not enjoy the feeling of pain we receive when attempting to overcome our weaknesses. The feeling of pain is so deep that we avoid it at all costs.

For me to become this new, confident person I always wanted to be, I knew I had to be great at losing weight. Like Charles, I enjoyed working on my strengths. For example, in the beginning of my journey, leaving the gym full of sweat after an intense weight-lifting workout gave me a feeling of enjoyment. Also, I was good at making healthy food choices during the week, before the weekend approached. You must understand, because of a steady practice with my strengths I became really good at adapting to this new lifestyle. On the other hand, my weaknesses involved committing to my cardio regimen and sticking to my eating routines on the weekends. At the end of the week when it was time to weigh in, I found I had either lost only a few pounds or none at all. I knew what my weaknesses were, but I dreaded the feeling I'd surely experience when I had to put those weaknesses to the test.

After experiencing inconsistent weight-loss results week after week, I finally had "enough" and decided to start putting more attention on fixing my flaws. First, I made a commitment to perform all of my cardio workouts for the week. Second, I committed to a steady eating regimen both during the week and the weekends. Yes, I must admit it sucked staying on the treadmill for the whole duration. I didn't really enjoy prepping my meals each Friday. But I knew it had to be done for me to consistently lose weight.

After committing to striking down my weaknesses and advancing through the grueling week, it was time to step on the scale. I did not know what to expect; I was just hoping for positive results. I took off all my clothes and stepped on the scale. To my amazement, I realized I lost more weight that week than any previous weeks during my journey. My eyes lit up when I finally learned the best lesson for me in becoming great at achieving weight loss—consistently practice and become better at the activities where I don't excel. Over the next four weeks, I routinely completed my cardio regimen and made smart food choices. The activities I once viewed as painful, were now looked upon as actual needs. I call them needs because every part of the process has to be efficient for you to achieve successful weight loss. I finally understood that for me to be great at losing weight, I MUST improve upon my weaknesses. Please understand that you do not have to be a super star in all areas when dealing with the weight-loss process, but you have to be at least efficient enough to get the job done. For example, Charles does not have to be great at rebounding, but he does have to be good enough to not let reboundings set him up for failure.

People who are amazed by my weight-loss story and transformation often ask how I learned to stay consistent. I give a simple answer every time. I had to follow through with meal prep when I didn't feel like it, exercise when I was tired, and say "no" to desserts, even when they were calling my name. I did anything and everything that was needed to become successful at losing weight. I practiced turning those weaknesses into strengths over and over until there were no more faults in my arsenal. The funny thing is that so many people look at both my commitment to exercise and my eating patterns and think I make it seem so simple. It only looks easy because of the constant and consistent time I invest to become better.

It is not unlike my days playing in the NFL. The difference I saw between average players and great players was their approach in dealing with consistent mistakes. NFL athletes who are considered the best at their sport have coaches because they have weaknesses. You show me a player that is perfect with no flaws, and I will show you Jesus. It is impossible to be successful in every area, but you can always become better.

For example, look at how well you do your job or learned how to do your job. I'll bet in the early days you were not comfortable with every duty and are probably still not great at every aspect. Like most people, you undoubtedly work five days a week and carry out your job responsibilities day after day. The difference between weight loss and your job is that your supervisor at the workplace expects you to learn and grow as time goes on. It is understood that you will make mistakes, but you are expected to become more knowledgeable and proficient with time. If you do not show improvement, I am sure you will not last long as an employee. In order for a business to succeed, it must demand time and efficient effort. I treat myself and my clients that I mentor in the same manner.

Yes, you will make bad decisions when learning how to lose weight effectively, but you will work on your difficulties so you can become productive every day. It is normal to experience weaknesses at the start of your weight-loss journey, but it is not okay if you do not know how to correct them. You cannot continue to make wrong decisions. A long time ago, one of my great football coaches shared with me two reasons as to why people continue to make the same mistakes after being corrected—either they are stupid or they don't care. I am pretty sure if you are reading this book, you are intelligent. You just have to care more about the choices you are making.

It's time to take pride in your efforts and make the constant choice to improve the flaws in your game to become great at losing weight. So, look at the weaknesses in your weight-loss process and ask yourself in which areas you are falling behind. Here are some, to name a few: planning, meal prepping, eating every three hours, considering recipe options, and enjoying your workout routines. Do you shy away from executing certain activities because you are not good with that particular action or task? Do you need some training on exactly how to properly execute a particular activity? Only you know the answers to your questions. It's now time to overcome those weaknesses.

Journaling: What's Your Story?

Chapter 24: How to Become Great at Weight Loss

1. What are the weaknesses that are stopping you from being great at weight loss?

2. How will you overcome these weaknesses?

3. Who is coaching you through your weight-loss journey?

If you need coaching to help you to become great at weight loss, please go to: www.TheTPexperience.com

Chapter 25: Adapting Through The Process

You have read and understood the steps to my weight-loss formula. Executing the formula with consistency will only guide you in the right direction. The formula is your navigational system to reach your destination. Have you ever gone on a road trip for a vacation or to visit family? Throughout the journey you may encounter unexpected road bumps. You may have to take detours because of blocked roads due to construction. During the traveling process it is possible to get a flat tire. The road traveled has curves, hills, dips, and rough uneven pavement. Halfway through your trip you find traffic to be backed up for miles, costing you hours and putting you way behind schedule. The navigational system never points out these encounters when pulling up the directions, right?

Everything you run across during your drive is just a part of the process that comes with finally reaching your destination. When we experience these setbacks, we don't turn around and go back home. We keep moving in the right direction until the voice on our navigational system states we have arrived. This is the approach you must take, both when starting and continuing, on your own fitness journey.

Through all my years of being on this earth I have never heard someone say, "I want to get in shape, but I need my schedule to never change, workouts to always be fun and easy, nutritious food to taste as good as the unhealthy foods, be able to only exercise outside during perfect weather, and begin my journey with no disruptions." We start off by stating we want to hit our goals and that we are ready for change.

To achieve anything that is new and requires learning, understand you will have your good days and bad days. You will experience growing pains and tough times. It's just part of the process. The worst thing you can do during your journey is to turn around. Giving up on your journey will never get you closer to your goals. Traveling on your road trip and turning around because it requires a detour will never get you closer to your destination. Yes, the process may suck at times, and yes, there will be times you want to quit. I'd be lying to you if I said I never wanted to quit during my process of losing weight.

Imagine your journey as an annoying and uncomfortable bumpy road. We have already made up our mind that turning around is not an option. We are only faced with two other options.

We can grit our teeth and accept the uncomfortable bumpy road. Looking for another route that may offer a smoother ride would be the other option. Those were the choices I had when facing adversity. My smoother roads were changing my exercise routine because I quickly became bored. My smoother roads were changing my meal options because the food, over time, was not pleasurable to consume.

We tend to act more on our feelings rather than logic. Hence, why we do things we feel like doing instead of the things we know we should be doing? This concept is very similar to our approach when starting our fitness journey. Have you ever prolonged your start date because the feeling of pain enters your mind? Do you experience the feeling of pain because you attempted to lose weight and failed every time? For example, you may have chosen a meal plan or meal replacement shake system that worked for a friend or family member. After following the strategy for a few days you find yourself not fascinated with their plan. You may have purchased a fitness video you observed on television, but the exercises painfully bothered your knees and back.

One thing I learned through my own weight-loss experience and witnessing so many others' is that we all have different tastes in what we enjoy or dislike. We all adapt differently when confronted with adversity, and that's what makes us all unique. Not everyone likes the same things, but you have to find a routine that you do enjoy. One thing we all share are the feelings of pleasure and pain.

Pain and Pleasure

As humans, we enjoy activities that bring us feelings of pleasure and joy. The activity alone does not create these particular feelings. Our experience during the activity creates the feeling of pleasure. Think about a sport, video game, television show, movie, or any activity you enjoy. During the activity you experienced the emotion of joy and because of that experience you created a habit of repeating the activity over and over again. You are confident knowing you will experience emotions of pleasure when actively performing this activity; you seldom procrastinate performing the task.

Now let's think about an activity that carries a feeling of pain. It may be going to a job you hate, cleaning your house, or seeing certain family members you don't get along with. One activity I always pushed away from and brought me pain was the act of ironing my school clothes. My mother forced me to iron all my uniform school clothes every Sunday at a young age. I had to iron five shirts and five pairs of pants. This process took me an hour, and I disliked every minute of it. Every Sunday I procrastinated and looked for distractions until my mother threatened me to iron my clothes before she put me on punishment. Understand that ironing itself is not painful, but my experience during the whole ironing process was very painful. You may not experience pain when ironing, so we may not share the same feeling with that certain activity. It is the same as if I enjoy running and experience pleasure. You may hate running and experience pain throughout the activity. It is important that you find a process that contains a proven system to follow.

It is more important to find a proven system that does not spark a dreadful feeling. For example, I witness women that can walk on the treadmill for hours and enjoy every minute of it. If that was the only way I was told I had to lose my weight, I know for sure I would have quit after the first day. Everyone states the phrase, "I want to make a lifestyle change." You must understand that the lifestyle change must not only provide you with a "change." It also must also provide you with a change that offers enjoyment to you. It's important to practice a gratifying process that you can transform into lifelong habits.

On your weight-loss journey it is essential to explore different styles of exercise and food options you enjoy, or at the least options that do not feel dreadful. If you don't like running, then don't run. If you don't like eating salads, then do not eat salads. Exploring new and alternative activities during the process is the secret to sustaining the feeling of excitement and pleasure.

Pleasure through Nutrition

Experiencing pleasure through nutrition, for many, is eating a big piece of cheesecake or having almost anything fried. Food feels like a drug to so many people because of the feeling we receive during every bite. I truly believe food is actually more addicting than drugs because food is offered everywhere you go on earth. If you want drugs, you have to find a drug dealer or a drug-infested neighborhood. We do not have to search far or long for food because it is in front of our face every day. There are food commercials, fast-food restaurants on almost every corner, and food billboards on the highway enticing us to get off at the exit. It seems like there are new dollar-deal menus every week encouraging us to buy these pleasurable foods we know are not healthy for our bodies. I understand the struggle to say no to these pleasures.

One of the common problems I hear from people I coach is that they are bored and get burned out with eating the food they cook. Once they reach this point, they start to fall into a deep, miserable state and begin dreading eating the meals they prepped for the day. After days or weeks of these terrible feelings, they start to break their healthy eating habits. They begin to insert the pleasurable unhealthy foods back in their diet. Once they begin to fall in love with the feeling of pleasure with their fried foods or fast food choices, they quit their journey.

One of the old sayings is, "You will only do what you know." If you were like me when I first started my weight-loss journey, I only knew how to cook chicken with one type of seasoning. I only knew one marinade I enjoyed that flavored my fish. The only veggies I cooked were green beans and broccoli. Over time, my taste buds grew tired of the same flavors. To be honest, the food had little flavor because my knowledge of how to incorporate spices and herbs was little to none.

Unfortunately, I did what anyone would do when they wanted something good to eat after a long day of work. I drove to my favorite pizza spot or burger joint. The worst part about going back to these pleasurable foods is that it increased my hatred for bland, healthy foods even more.

Growing up in my household, I was not the type of kid that hung around the kitchen and watched my mother cook dinner. I was either outside playing sports with friends or at football practice. Having little to no knowledge on how to cook limited my choices and hurt me when it was time for me to cook my own meals.

Cooking was very uncomfortable for me because I had little confidence in my abilities. When I was in college I tried cooking a few meals and they turned out to be horrible. My macaroni and cheese attempt was too creamy because I added too much milk. My ground turkey burger was way overcooked. If I had to pinpoint the reasons why my attempts failed, it was due to the incorrect measurements. In college I didn't own a measuring cup. I had to estimate the amount for a cup or a teaspoon, and a majority of the time my food turned out tasting awful. As I said before, I was not a very detailed person, and it showed with my cooking.

After eating the same boring seasoning over and over again, I knew it was time for a change if I wanted to keep my excitement and focus. Remember, we don't quit or give up. We simply find another way or another route. The other route I chose in order to enjoy my healthy food was to ask others for guidance. We all separate ourselves with our strengths and weaknesses. I had a few family members and friends that were talented in the kitchen. I learned simple and quick ways to spice up my lean meats to improve the taste. The Internet was also another route I chose to follow. I found more ways in which to prepare my healthy menu. I am a visual learner, so being able to watch YouTube videos was a home run for me.

One of my funniest moments learning how to cook was when I searched for new seasonings and spices. If you looked in my seasoning cupboard before I learned how to cook, you would have found salt, pepper, seasoning salt, and possibly garlic salt. The grocery shopping phase was the not-so-pleasurable part of learning how to cook. My runs to the grocery store were pathetic.

During my college days, I spent less than ten minutes strolling through the soda, chip, frozen dinner, and cereal aisles. Now that I had to find new items, I thought I would feel like I was a kid in an Easter egg hunt. Walking through the same aisles over and over again boiled my blood. It, literally, took me twenty to thirty minutes to find one item. I refused to ask for help because I didn't want to look like I was a rookie.

Over time, the treasure hunts for items became easier and easier. As time went on, I knew exactly where to go to find my seasonings and food items needed to cook my meals. Sometimes strangers asked me for help and I would show them as I poked my chest out with confidence. Over the years I learned to turn myself into a pretty good cook. Meal prepping is not painful anymore, and I enjoy the taste of the food I prepare.

Sometimes you must get out of your comfort zone to win on your fitness journey. Ask for help from others and feed off of their strengths. If you do not have others to count on for help, look online for easy recipes. Once you build confidence in your cooking abilities, I suggest you keep learning new ways to prepare your healthy meals. Over time, your menu choices will expand and you will enjoy your new lifestyle change of healthy eating.

Pleasure through Exercise

Many people who know me often hear me say that I have an attention deficit disorder when it comes to exercise. I often get bored quickly with exercise routines. I also didn't enjoy exercising in the gym for longer than one hour. During my one-hundred-pound weight-loss journey I've taken off large chunks of weight by incorporating different styles of exercise training. Some of these include: cross fit, weight training, road running, calisthenics, cardio, and high intensity interval training. Every exercise style increased my excitement to exercise because it was something new and different.

I recommend changing up your workout routine when needed if you see your motivation to exercise slowly disappearing. Changing your workout also helps to throw off the body from adapting to your routine. Now I have to admit, during the first few months of my journey, I couldn't perform and didn't enjoy cross fit exercises and road running. As I started to lose more weight and gain better cardio endurance, I was able to incorporate cross fit and running. Being able to perform exercises I could never image myself previously completing was a major emotional accomplishment for me.

The first time I ever completed my first pull-up was a game changer. Throughout college and the NFL I could never do a full pull-up. In the weight room I was strong and could easily bench-press well over 400 pounds. My teammates were able to perform pull-ups and I would just watch in awe. Pull-ups were just not an exercise for big, heavy guys. I remember my first pull-up like it was yesterday. I may have been five to seven months into my weight-loss journey and I had already lost sixty to seventy pounds.

In 2011, a friend of mine introduced me to the world of cross fit. He raved about how fun it was and described the rush felt when completing one of the workouts. The only rush I received after working out in the past was the rush to lie down. So I took him on his offer to try one of his workouts. He e-mailed me the workout and I noticed one of the exercises was—you guessed it—pull-ups! I knew for a fact that was one exercise I could not complete. I decided to complete the majority of the workout; I would just skip the pull-ups.

During the workout I enjoyed completing exercises for time because I was able to compete against myself. I finished all the exercises except the pull-ups. It seemed like the pull-up bar was looking at me and I asked myself, *"Who am I kidding?"* First, I didn't want to try to pull myself up and embarrass myself in front of the others in the gym. Second, I figured my body was so tired from the exercises I'd already done, there was no way I could do a pull-up. I slowly walked over to the pull-up bar and grabbed it with two hands.

Since I was six foot seven inches, I didn't have to jump like others because I was so tall. Once I had a good grip, I hung onto the bar with my knees bent so my feet would not touch the ground. My back muscles started to squeeze intensely as I started to pull myself up. I could not believe that I was actually doing this and reached my chin over the bar. I jumped off the bar, looking around to see if anybody was watching me. My smile went from ear to ear and right then I knew my physical ability was changing before my eyes.

To my surprise after starting this journey I began to enjoy running. Yes, I said running. As you learned earlier, from my childhood and college days, running was my kryptonite. I would almost rather die or settle for being unhealthy if I was told the only way I could lose weight was by running. My routine for cardio was riding the elliptical or walking uphill on the treadmill. This suddenly changed when my younger brother Kevin introduced me to road running. Kevin enjoyed running outside, and I always told him he was insane. He invited me to go running with him many times and I'd look at him like he had lost his mind.

One cool, windy day I was lacing up my shoes before heading to the gym to work on the cardio machines. This typical light day for me was only about burning a few calories. Kevin stopped me at the front door before leaving and asked if I'd go running with him. He explained that we would only run ten minutes one way and then turn around and come back. Around that time I was weighing just below 300 pounds.

Thoughts of running during football conditioning jumped into my head and misery was written all over my face. I ultimately agreed to step out of my comfort zone and give it a try. We stepped outside and I started my big-man shuffle. The big-man shuffle is when you trot instead of jog. The big-man shuffle speed is between a power walk and light jog. I continued my shuffle for the first ten minutes. When we turned around I noticed I was not as tired as I expected. I decided to turn my shuffle into a slightly faster jog and it felt incredible. To be able to run and not be out of breath was a new and invigorating feeling for me. We returned home, and I sat down on the porch, realizing what I just did. I could not believe I actually enjoyed the run and was planning on doing it again the next day.

Road running helped me to lose another thirty pounds. I still enjoy road running because it helps me to meditate and clear my mind. During your weight-loss journey you will also experience these times of enjoyment and accomplishment. To achieve these feelings you must step out of your comfort zone and try new things. You never know what activities may become a part of your new life.

Journaling: What's Your Story?

Chapter 25: Adapting Through the Process

1. What part of the process do you dislike most? (Check all that apply)
   □ Nutrition or
   □ Exercise

2. What actions will you take to make the process much more enjoyable?

3. Have you ever reached a proud moment with your physical progress through exercise?

4. What new exercise routine or concept will you try if you become bored with your current routine?

5. Are you tired of eating the same boring food and need more options? ____Yes or ____No. If yes, explain why.

Visit: www.TheTPexperience.com

Chapter 26: Measuring Your Activity

Over the past several years coaching others and sharing advice regarding weight loss, I've noticed that many people don't measure their activity. It would suck to work your butt off every day in the gym, be strict with your diet, and then find out you had only lost one pound during a five-week span. The feeling would be even more devastating once you found out the small weight loss was due to consuming too many or too little calories daily. One small tweak here and there can make big changes with your results.

There are many ways we can measure our results on a weekly or monthly basis. You can use the scale, pictures, clothes, or measuring tape. All of these tools are great ways to measure because everyone loses weight differently, depending on their body type. For example, I gain muscle mass quickly and it can throw off my weight-loss numbers when measuring on the scale. At times the scale discouraged me, and on any given day, I knew my weight would fluctuate because of the gallon of water I drank or the amount of sodium I consumed. I could never pinpoint why, but I knew if I wanted to sustain my high level of excitement, I needed another way to show my results.

Pictures

We are visual creatures, don't you agree? Photographs and pictures provide incentives for many people to begin their weight-loss journey. You may look at photos taken while you were on vacation or at a party. You will then ask yourself the most important question of how you have let yourself go. The pictures bring us out of our denial frame of mind and help us make a decision to change our ways.

So many of us (including me) cover our bodies with clothes so we don't have to look at its flaws. We begin to avoid the problem and cover up with big, baggy clothes. If pictures can motivate us to make a change, they can also motivate us to sustain excitement along our journey.

I took photographs with just my underwear on—from the front, sides, and the back. I compared these pictures every month so I could notice the change in my body composition. My monthly updated pictures showed my stomach shrinking, my fat rolls disappearing, and my cheeks and neck shrinking. The pictures motivated me to keep going on my journey and helped me to increase my level of discipline. They say a picture is worth a thousand words. The photos I took of myself were telling me a thousand times to keep going.

Measuring tape

I used a measuring tape to measure my waist every three weeks. I measured by using my bellybutton as the mark to consistently measure at the same position. Pinpointing different spots on the same body part may give you inaccurate results. The key is to make sure you are using the same spot every time to measure the different parts of your body. The common body parts to measure are the back, chest, waist, hips, and thighs. These are your biggest body parts and tend to hold the majority of your body fat. Grab a notebook and date your measurements. Measuring your back and chest may become difficult, so ask a friend or family member for assistance to gain accurate measurements. I measured the same spot two or three times to make sure my measurements were the same. If you need help with how to properly measure, search for videos or articles online.

Your clothes

Through my years of coaching I have come across so many people that worry about how their clothes fit, rather than how much they weigh. I understand that we are generally more unhappy with the way we look than how much we weigh. The look is what frightens us or makes us unhappy with our self-image. So, it's a great idea to use clothes as another measurement tool on your weight-loss journey.

When dealing with weight gain or loss, the clothes never lie. Our clothes can help us in many ways, not just by covering our bodies. Clothes can help us with self-awareness when we are in a state of denial. There were many times I noticed whether or not I was gaining or losing weight by how my clothes fit. In my closet I own many tailored shirts and pants. There were times when my pants fit looser and times they fit tighter. I am sure you have noticed this a few times in your own life.

I used clothes as another way to motivate me on my journey. When I first started losing weight I wore a 5xl shirt. One of my favorite stores to shop is Macy's. They carry a variety of big and tall clothes. The problem was I would find a shirt I really loved and it would always be a size too small. Macy's carried many styles in sizes of 2xl or 3xl. So, I made it my goal to fit into one of those shirts. I bought a 3xl shirt that I knew I couldn't squeeze into at the time and hung it on my closet door. I put the shirt on once a month and noticed how it felt looser each month. This shirt was my personal motivation because, once I knew I could fit into it comfortably, my options to buy clothes shot to another level. Once I hit below 280 pounds, I was able to fit into the shirt quite comfortably. It was a momentous day was a huge game changer for me!

You may be in the situation where you don't enjoy shopping for clothes. I advise you to pick something out of your closet or purchase an item one size smaller than you currently can wear. Hang it up somewhere noticeable so you can look at it every single day.

You may already have lots of clothes in your closet that don't fit anymore since gaining your weight. If so, hang up just one of these items to help motivate you. This will remind you why you are fighting on your journey. Once you are able to fit in the smaller size, repeat the process. Buy another piece of clothing (or choose an existing item) that is a smaller size than you currently wear until you hit your goal size.

The scale

The word "scale" is a troubling word for so many. The scale can be a gift and a curse. I first want to breakdown the purpose of the scale. The scale's purpose is to measure four things that make up your body's weight: your bones, muscles, water, and fat. As we may know, our body is made up mostly of water (55 to 60 percent). The scale cannot tell us what percentage of our weight is from bones, muscles, or fat. Losing weight can become very tricky because we may not know exactly what we are losing. We hopefully know that we will not lose the weight of our bones. We will only gain or lose the weight of water, muscle tissue, or body fat. In training and coaching clients, over the years, I find they all encounter different experiences with the scale. I have learned there are two types of people when dealing with the scale.

1. The avoider

Some of my clients are terrified to weigh themselves because they are afraid of the number that appears. They went through so many bad experiences with past weight-loss attempts, they dread stepping on the scale. They would rather avoid the scale so they can avoid disappointment. These clients treat their weight like so many treat their bills. Have you ever retrieved your mail and noticed that one of the items was a bill? Instead of looking at your bill to acknowledge the damage you owe, you throw it into a pile with your other bills and take care of it later. The bill is later forgotten and you receive late payment notices. You continue to avoid the late notices until you are threatened that either your bill will be sent to collections or your service will be disconnected. You now have to make a decision and you are forced to act on paying the bill.

Many clients I meet for the first time encounter this same type of scenario when I ask them to step on the scale. They say they have not weighed themselves in months. Once they read the numbers on the scale, they are in shock and can't believe they've gained so much weight.

The lengthy avoidance and unawareness of knowing how much you weigh may promote the same feeling a person may have when looking at their credit card statement. They carelessly used their credit card to purchase items and are not aware of the damage. If you feel this is you, then look at your weight number like it's a credit card bill you must pay off. To pay off the debt we must make adjustments with our habits and daily activities. We stop spending money on restaurants, the mall, and vacations.

We also discontinue making any more purchases that will slow down our process to pay off the bill. All of a sudden you buy things you need and not things you want. You may have to work overtime or find an additional part-time job to pay off the bill. The principles and desires to change are the same principles and desires when dealing with weight loss.

During the weight-loss process we have to cut back on high-calorie foods that are helping your body store fat. You make a choice to burn more energy with exercise routines throughout the week. As you go along with these new habits you realize you are chipping away at the weight like you do when chipping away to lessen the credit card bill. It takes discipline and steady focus on your goal to pay off the credit card bill and to lose weight. You may choose to commit to paying one-hundred dollars a month towards the credit card debt. You may choose to commit to lose eight to ten pounds a month on your weight-loss journey.

The moral of this comparison is to sacrifice and make the necessary adjustments to reach your goal numbers. Own up to your actions that lead to the number you now see on your scale. It is just a number, and you have full control to make the number change.

The second type of scale avoider would rather not step on the scale at all during their journey because they are scared of their results. As a trainer at a gym years ago, I remember meeting a woman that had already been on her fitness journey for several weeks. I asked her how much weight she had lost so far and she responded by saying, "I don't know." She explained that she had not stepped on the scale since starting her journey. Her past experiences regarding weight-loss attempts and the scale crumpled her spirits. I then asked her, "What do you do to measure your results?" She replied, "I don't do anything." I told her that I would like to help her get over her fear of the scale and change her approach to it. She agreed to meet with me the next morning to talk.

The next morning arrived and we met in my office to come up with a solution to her problem. We talked for an hour, and I learned that she had a business marketing background. We talked about marketing for the majority of the conversation, and at one point what stood out to me was her mentioning how she determined the most effective marketing strategy.

A business owner may use several different marketing plans, but they must measure which one is most effective and which one is not as effective. A light bulb went off in my head and I explained the similarities between marketing processes and losing weight. In business, the owner asks every client how they heard about their services in order to determine which marketing plan is producing the best results.

In weight loss one of the ways you can measure your exercise and nutrition activity is by using a scale. If you are not losing weight, then you might need to change or increase the energy used during exercise. Your nutrition calories may be too high or too low for consistent weight loss. I told this woman to use her scale to measure her activity. Change your purpose for your scale and it will change your feelings towards the scale.

At first, her purpose for using the scale was in hoping it would display the number she wished to see. Instead, you should use the scale as a way to understand how your body processed the food you put in your body and how your body reacted to your exercise routine. I asked her, "Would you recommend business owners use the same advertising plan that is not creating the results they expect?" She quickly replied "no." I asked, "How would these owners know, if they didn't measure the results?"

My last question to her was, "Why would you consistently exercise and eat a certain way without knowing if it is creating the results you expect?" She looked at me strangely and couldn't give me an answer. At the end of our talk she expressed that she understood the importance of measuring her results. Going forward, she did use the scale to make sure her exercise and nutrition practices were giving her the results she desired. Remember, small tweaks can make big changes with your weight loss.

2. The obsessor

On the other side of the coin I have experienced coaching clients who have the addictive habit of weighing themselves every morning. Weighing yourself everyday can become harmful in terms of dealing with your motivation. I was a person that weighed every morning because I was curious how much my weight would change daily. There were good days and there were bad days. If you weigh yourself everyday like I did, then you may understand those bad days. The days I lost weight I would attack my challenges and obstacles with a great inspiring attitude. The days I didn't lose weight, my attitude dropped and my day was ruined.

The scale can definitely alter your attitude. Throughout your weight-loss journey your attitude must stay in the positive zone. To be truly honest, on the days I didn't lose weight, I strayed from my meal plan. I was so upset with the number displayed on the scale, I looked toward food for comfort. So many times I told myself, "I didn't lose weight today anyway, so why would this bacon cheeseburger hurt?" These are the days we must avoid if we want to reach our weight-loss goals.

As weeks went by, I realized that weighing myself everyday was not emotionally good for me. One day I stepped on the scale and my weight had jumped up two pounds from the previous day. My mood changed dramatically, and I wanted to throw my scale against the wall. My frustration grew stronger and stronger by the hour. I could not understand how I could gain two pounds after eating healthy and completing difficult exercises the night before.

Usually when I am stuck for an answer, I research online for answers. I learned that our weight may fluctuate and that weighing yourself everyday may not be healthy for the mind. The article recommended weighing yourself once a week in the morning before your first meal. After reading the article, I figured I'd give it a shot. I chose to weigh myself every Saturday morning because it helped me to stay on my eating regimen on Friday nights. As we know, Friday nights hanging out with friends or eating out at restaurants for entertainment can throw you off your diet.

During the week I put my scale under my bed so I would not be tempted to automatically step on it. This weigh-in routine worked wonders for me; I began to lose weight weekly, and my motivation increased by the week. If you are a person that is dealing with this problem, change your routine and pick one day each week to weigh yourself—hide your scale during the week, if needed.

Journaling: What's Your Story?

Chapter 26: Measuring Your Activity

1. How do you measure your results? (Check all that apply)
   □ Measuring tape
   □ Scale
   □ Clothes
   □ Pictures

2. Have you ever let the disappointing numbers on the scale destroy your motivation?
   ____Yes or ___No. If yes, explain why.

   ____
   ____
   ____
   ____
   ____
   ____

3. When using the scale to measure your results, would you consider yourself an:

   □ Avoider
   or
   □ Obsessor

Chapter 27: "You Look Great" Trap

Your desire to change your life is the reason why you started this journey. Your desire to become happier and uplift your self-image was the driving force you needed to finally commit to your plan. Traveling along your fitness journey you will encounter a trap that will either stop your momentum or derail you from your routine. The "you look great" trap has destroyed so many people from hitting their end goals. So, you may be wondering what the "you look great" trap actually is.

Let me explain this trap through my own experience. After losing the first fifty pounds on my weight-loss journey, my appearance changed dramatically. My choice of both style and size of clothes provided the first big change in my appearance. When I weighed 350 pounds, I bought most of my clothing from the big and tall section. I wore a size 5xl or 6xl shirts and a size 50-52 in jeans. The fit was big and baggy so I could hide my big belly and other body parts that I was not proud to show. Once my weight dropped below 300 pounds, I was able to finally fit into3xl shirts.

Weighing less than 300 pounds, my stomach shrunk down tremendously and wearing tight-fitting shirts was no problem. The next appearance that stood out was the slimming of my cheeks and neck. The fat around my face slimmed down and I was able to see my jaw line and cheekbones. Wearing clothes that fit nicely helped increase my confidence, and I was finally enjoying how my clothes fit my body.

I noticed that the new appearance helped me to receive attention from the ladies. Everything was going well with my weight-loss journey. My exercise routine and nutrition plan were in sync. The numbers on the scale were dropping every week, and I was very confident that I would finally reach my end goal. My end goal was not to reach a certain weight or to fit into a certain size. My end goal was to walk into a water park and take off my shirt with full confidence.

I had never even been to a water park, so I wanted to experience the feeling of walking around without thinking that people were laughing at my body—finally being able to stroll through the water park without my belly bouncing up and down. This was my personal goal, and

I knew I would never have a high self-image until I completed this goal. My personal goal was my motivator to keep going and never stop.

This concept suddenly changed when people started to tell me how great I looked. I heard such comments as, "You are going to be too skinny," and "You look great as you are right now." I want to touch on the "you are going to be too skinny" statement. My mother always told me she liked how I looked and that I didn't need to lose any more weight. I love my mother dearly, but I also know she has only seen her baby boy as heavy set with plump cheeks. Having her see my new appearance was new to her, but it wasn't about her or her needs. I know her heart was in the right place, but I had to remember this was my mission and my happiness.

My family and friends complimented me on how much weight I lost. I would boast, at times, sharing with them how much I lost because it felt so good hearing those compliments. Family members I had not seen in years told me that I didn't need to lose any more weight. Hearing these comments on social media, my workplace, or at events was starting to ruin the personal goals I had in mind. I started to think that maybe everyone was right; I didn't need to lose more weight. I began to listen to others' opinions, instead of what I wanted for my life.

Many times we let the criticism and opinions of others run our lives. All of those opinions surely distracted me from my course. The thought of settling began to seep into my routine. My desire and fire was slowly burning out, and I noticed it was hard to find motivation to complete my routine. It started with going through the motions in my workouts. In addition, my eating habits were terrible. The numbers on the scale were stagnant, and I was okay with that. The worst thing that could have happened just happened. Again I let others' opinions destroy what I wanted most for myself.

My slump lasted a few weeks and the old Terrance started to creep back into my life. Fast-food runs, late-night eating, and desserts were in my nutrition rotation. I lost my purpose and my motivation. You will encounter these moments when you feel like your motivation is slowly dying inside you. One of my goals I wrote down when beginning my journey was to finish what I started. I looked in the mirror and asked myself, "Do I want to quit on another task? Are you truly satisfied with the end result? Are you ready to settle again for others?"

That night I went back to my dry erase board and went through my formula. I noticed I wasn't planning, committing, winning, or repeating the last few weeks. When you are in a slump, it feels like it is hard to get back on track. Getting up to go to the gym is difficult. Meal prepping seems impossible. There is only one way to get out of your weight-loss slump.

To get out of the slump you must build positive momentum. Your small wins include your decisions that will, in turn, create momentum and spark your motivation. Let go of the past setbacks and control your next move. We all make mistakes; distractions will attack you. Always remember to fall back to the formula and do not stop until you reach your end goal.

Journaling: What's Your Story?

Chapter 27: "You Look Great" Trap

1. Have you ever been a victim of this trap? ____ Yes or ____ No. Share your story.

____

____

____

____

____

____

____

2. How will you protect yourself from the trap in the future?

____

____

____

____

____

____

____

Chapter 28: How Does The Journey End?

I want to say "sorry" now in advance, because this journey never really ends. Your goals may have been reached but the journey continues. Part of the journey is making the right decisions that are best for your health and self-image. This weight-loss journey was never ultimately about losing weight. Losing your weight just came along with the process of making the right decisions—to eat less fast food, exercise, and control your emotions. I have mentioned many times in this book that this battle is about keeping your focus and making the right decisions.

One of the hardest challenges in human existence is to master self. Mastering self is an ongoing process and the journey never ends. The reason it never ends is because life's distractions entice you to make the wrong decisions. Your decisions determine the outcome for everything you do in life. In the beginning you may have viewed losing weight as pain or a battle you could not beat. Once you finally accomplish your goals, the journey will be seen as an achievement under your belt. Your outlook dealing with exercise and nutrition will be totally different compared to your first day on your journey.

I often tell people that the fat boy is still inside of me and I still enjoy desserts. I just know how to keep this fat boy inside me locked up. I let him out to the world at times when I want to enjoy food, but I am fully aware of when to lock him right back up again. Remember, it is only a fight if you let it become your struggle. I don't let my old ways and habits fight with my ultimate goals. You will never fall deeply back into your old habits once you understand your weaknesses and know how not to let them defeat you. Since I understand that desserts are my weakness, I know when to bring them into my life and when to avoid them. Again, it's your journey and you are in full control of the path you take.

Becoming the example

Through your journey you will become the inspiration and the example for others to follow. You will inspire your spouse, family, friends, and strangers with your story. When starting my journey I asked others to jump on board with me. I learned that others will start their journey when they are willing and ready. You can push and shove to motivate them to begin but most times it will push them further away. If you really want to inspire others, then you must inspire with your actions. The majority of the time others will become inspired with what they see. Your determination and results will help others to finally get out of their comfort zone.

There is no better feeling knowing that what you are giving them will change their life forever. Your friends and family will admire you and ask for advice. People will want to know about your secret or quick fix. Tell your story to instill value in their lives. Share with others how you overcame your failures and the times you wanted to throw in the towel. Share how you committed to your plan and followed a system that worked for you. You will become the example that others need to see for them to follow in your footsteps. I hope my story and proven system instilled value into your life. Enjoy the journey.

Chapter 28: How Does the Journey End?

Now you have the formula and the mindset it takes to reach your goals.

Visit www.TheTPexperience.com to invest in his proven exercise program, nutrition program, and other programs that will help you to enjoy the journey.

About the Author

Terrance Pennington

Author/Life Coach/Professional Speaker/Fitness Expert

Terrance Pennington was born in Los Angeles, California. A former NFL football player, Pennington was the 2006 seventh-round draft pick for the Buffalo Bills. He also played for the Atlanta Falcons and New York Giants. After leaving the NFL, Terrance was inspired to launch his own company, "The TP Experience," which specializes in personal training, motivational speaking, and result-producing life coaching.

Terrance has always had the passion and desire to help people. His new book, *Terrance Pennington's Play-by-Play: Coaching You Through His Weight-Loss Journey,* was recently released. Terrance provides the readers with timeless principles on how he was able to lose one-hundred pounds and change his entire lifestyle. Over the past few years he has devoted his life to helping others do the same. Terrance practices these principles and strategies every day and is living proof that they work. His success with teaching the "Play-by-Play System" helps participants become more efficient and proactive during their weight-loss transition.

As a successful fitness trainer and author, Terrance is also a highly sought after motivational speaker. He has been able to create a practical system that has helped hundreds to master their weight-loss goals and inspired them to live a healthier lifestyle. Due to his success, he has landed many opportunities to speak at colleges, universities, large corporations, churches, government, and non-profit agencies.

During his presentations, Terrance shares his motivational story and leaves his audience with an uplifting spirit that proves to them that they can truly reach their happiness and success. His message is shared with business leaders, single parents, teachers, and personal trainers. People throughout the world are improving their quality of life by following Terrance's simple techniques in his books and training programs.

Terrance strongly believes that motivation comes from within. He prides himself on being transparent and authentic, making him relatable to his audience. He strongly believes that we all are born winners, but it's our job to develop the winning mentality through constant practice.

Terrance's attended the University of New Mexico where he pursued a degree in Business Management. He currently lives in Murfreesboro, Tennessee, with his wife.

For additional copies of

Play-by-Play: Coaching You Through His Weight-Loss Formula

ORDER FORM

NAME: ______________________________

ADDRESS: ______________________________

CITY: ____________________ **STATE:** __________ **ZIP CODE:** __________

PHONE: (H) ____________________ **(C)** ____________________

E-MAIL ADDRESS: ______________________________

(Please allow 1 - 2 weeks for delivery.)			
Qty.	**Product Description**	Unit Cost	Total $
	Play-by-Play: Coaching You Through His Weight-Loss Formula	$19.95	
		Total Order	**$**
		Shipping & Handling	**$3.50**
	Tennessee Sales Taxes:		**$. 98**
		Grand Total	**$**

METHOD OF PAYMENT ☐ **CASH** ☐**CHECK** ☐ **MONEYORDER**

MAKE CHECK PAYABLE TO: The TP Experience LLC

Address: P.O. Box P.O. Box 10342, 2255 Memorial Boulevard, Murfreesboro, TN 37129

Credit Card ☐VISA ☐MasterCard

Number: ______________________________ **Exp.**__________

Signature______________________________ **CVC:** __________

E-mail: Terrancepennington@outlook.com **Website:** www.TheTPexperience.com

Phone: 615-513-5555